FLOOD, FIRE
AND A
SUPERSTORM

MARTY INGRAM

outskirts
press

Dedication

This book is dedicated to the brave members of the Point Breeze Fire Department (PBFD), who protect their community on the Rockaway peninsula with heroism and dedication. I will always refer to them as "the *core group*." Without them, the success of our struggles within Superstorm Sandy would not have been possible. I would also like to dedicate this book to all who have perished in hurricanes and fires and in the September 11, 2001 attacks.

Acknowledgements

AFTER THE STRUGGLES and challenges of Superstorm Sandy receded nearly a year after the event, many relatives and friends encouraged me to write this book. Upon hearing some of these tales as bedtime stories, my grandkids strongly recommended that I write a book about Hurricane Sandy. My good friend and fellow member of the Point Breeze Fire Department (PBFD) also convinced me that I needed to write about the experience from my unique perspective. As emergency responders we are trained regarding how to maintain our cool during the event, but none of us are trained how to handle ourselves in the aftermath. As a person and a neophyte writer I hit a brick wall which was much more than writer's block. I think I may have had a touch of Post-Traumatic Stress Disorder (PTSD). Finally, in 2020, all obstacles disappeared and the words began to fall into place. Ironically it happened during yet another disaster, the Pandemic of Covid 19.

I owe a tremendous debt of gratitude to my wife, Nancy, for her constant support, encouragement and editorial skills. My brother John, a recently retired New York State Supreme Court Judge contributed his sixty plus years' experience as a volunteer member of the PBFD and his superb editorial skills to make this book happen. My good friend, Sebastian Danese, aka Sea Bass, author of "The Battle for Breezy Point," offered his technical writing expertise. Like all of the books written about the Civil War, we both knew that one book was not enough to cover the enormity of Superstorm Sandy. During the night of the fire and subsequent recovery Sea Bass and I stood together in pursuit of a positive outcome. It is only natural that we help each other in telling our story.

Tim Dufficy, another member of the PBFD and a constant resource during the fire and recovery, offered endless assistance. Many people helped me greatly in navigating the turbulent waters in search of a publisher for this work.

My daughter, Erin Adams, and sons, Christopher, MJ, and Brendan Ingram also provided keen insight and donated their valuable time to provide editorial support for the development of the book. My neighbor and lifetime friend Mary Elizabeth Smith, a founding member of the Breezy Point Historical Society, spent many hours of review in helping me to finalize the package and to find a publisher. Lee Rosenzweig, an established author, provided valuable assistance in finding a publisher. I would also like to thank past editor of The Rockaway Wave, Howard Schwach and the present editor of the paper, Mark Healy, for their technical expertise. Past PBFD Chief Kurt Bruder and his sister, Jeanne, also provided valuable assistance in making this book a reality. I would like to thank Mike Archer for his outstanding advice and technical expertise. He is also an author and a TV news executive and producer in the Detroit, New York, and Philadelphia areas. Stephan "Butch" Moran was very helpful in providing photographs.

The last "angel" to appear came at the end. Her wings were working properly but her leg was in a cast. Her limited mobility allowed her an enormous amount of time to dedicate to formatting, editing, and arranging photo layouts. She was an excellent sounding board. Without Aggie Ferencz this book would have never existed.

Foreword

THE DAYS FOLLOWING the destruction of Superstorm Sandy which ravaged my home, office and entire community became mostly a blur, but to this day, the voice of Erin Ingram on the other side of the phone is still perfectly clear. Her words still echo in my ear today: "My father is alive and safe." I fell to the ground and thanked God for the words I needed to hear. Whether Marty knew it or not, on that day, he and his family helped provide the hope and strength I would need to continue in my work.

LESS THAN A year prior to the storm, Marty and I quickly became friends following my election. Breezy Point was a community I was still getting to know—one that truly embodied the spirit of connectivity and brotherhood. The Point Breeze Volunteer Fire Department was already a family to me--whether it was discussing how to aid recruitment, support state funding, was simply riding the trucks, or drinking a beverage with the crew--I loved every moment I spent with Marty and the PBFD crew.

IN THE DAYS leading up to the storm, my team and I did everything we could to help prepare our community for the wrath that was about to hit. At approximately 4:00 pm on October 29th, 2012, I made my final stop at the Point Breeze Volunteer Fire Department house, prior to sheltering in my own home. On Sunday, the station was strewn with volunteers sleeping on cots and mattresses after their work throughout the night. Others were already preparing for the next wave. What comforted the brave volunteers was the same force that calmed me, the confident and steadfast leadership of Chief Marty Ingram. I knew what he was about to face and I needed to give Marty one last hug to reassure him, but more importantly, to reassure me!

REPRESENTING THE NEIGHBORHOODS of southern Queens and Rockaway in the New York State Assembly was the greatest honor of my life, but nothing could have prepared me for the challenges Sandy would present. Friends helping friends, neighbor helping neighbor, the kindness of strangers from all over the world and the bravery shown by heroes like my great friend Chief Marty Ingram helped an entire community not only survive that night, but also thrive in the months ahead that carried us toward recovery. We weren't just a community anymore. We were a family, rebuilding the same home.

Phil Goldfeder
Former Member of NY Assembly
23rd District, Queens

Table of Contents

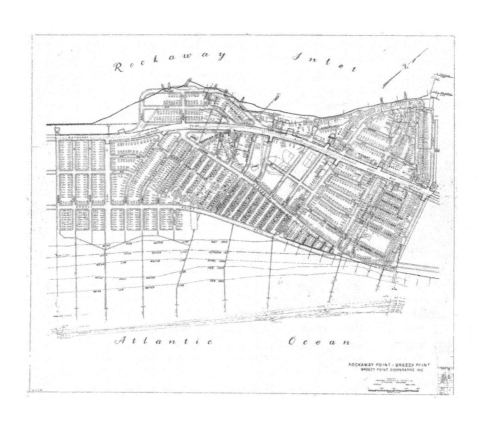

Rockaway Inlet

Atlantic Ocean

ROCKAWAY POINT - BREEZY POINT
BREEZY POINT COOPERATIVE INC.

CHAPTER 1

Trapped!

KURT BRUDER SHOUTED in my ear, "You have to evacuate now! You don't have a choice!" Kurt was Chief of the Point Breeze Volunteer Fire Department during the 9/11 attack and he was highly experienced. As a former chief, his primary role was to give assistance to me, the current chief, who was having a very bad day.

IT WAS OCTOBER 29, 2012 and Superstorm Sandy had just slammed into the New York metropolitan area. The community of Breezy Point, at the western tip of the Rockaway Peninsula, is a natural land barrier between the mainland of New York City and the Atlantic Ocean and it was totally inundated by Sandy's tidal surge.

BREEZY POINT IS a unique community built on sand with a few centrally located parking areas. On a normal day, people walk down narrow lanes to their homes, pulling wagons full of groceries. On this night, the tidal surge was being funneled through these tight spaces, thereby accelerating the water's velocity and, as a result, increasing its lethality. In a short time, we faced hurricane strength winds and floods that seemed of

biblical proportion. We had to abandon our firehouse and our fire trucks to seek higher and safer ground, carrying only our light tools, equipment, flashlights and radios, to set up shop in the building adjacent to the firehouse. This "clubhouse" was the highest ground in the neighborhood, and for those like myself, who lived through Hurricane Donna in 1960 we knew from experience it was the safest place to be. A few short moments, the overwhelming strength of "Superstorm Sandy" would prove that theory to be wrong.

THE WATER RAGED with all of nature's wrath and carried debris that turned the once-quiet neighborhood sidewalks into dangerous rapids. The water continued to rise to levels never witnessed before and at various locations was twenty feet deep. Like the fabled city of Atlantis, our community had slipped beneath the sea. In August 2011, Hurricane Irene was hyped to be a dangerous threat to the area by the media. But at the last moment, Irene changed direction and lost intensity. The damage from the storm was minimal. The end result caused many people to lose confidence in the media's ability to report severe weather. Many decided in advance that when the next storm was forecasted the evacuation orders would be ignored.

SHORTLY AFTER THE flood waters from the tidal surge inundated our area, we could see a few cars with their head and tail lights flashing on and off and could hear their horns honking above the howling wind. It looked to us like people had abandoned their homes and sought refuge in their cars. It was a dangerous place to seek sanctuary in the midst of a hurricane and flood. In the clubhouse we were monitoring the situation and developing plans to rescue them. We were making assessments and calculating the likelihood of a successful rescue. I needed to decide if they were safer in their cars or if we should develop a risky rescue plan. I knew full well that if my team became separated and couldn't return to the clubhouse, our likelihood for success during the rest of the night would be reduced and firefighters could die. As we were discussing our options, I noticed more and more cars were flashing their lights and honking their horns and that the on-off rate of the lights was the same in every car.

I thought it odd that so many people could orchestrate the same frequency of flashing lights. I began to suspect that this was a mechanical function of the cars and perhaps no one was in the vehicles after all. With a heavy heart I announced we were not going forward to attempt a rescue, potentially condemning countless neighbors and friends to drowning. The decision, of course, was met with some resistance but I explained to my men that if the people were in the cars, they were safer than trying to move about in the flooded debris-filled parking lot at the peak of the hurricane. Their lives, for the time being, were in the hands of God above.

FORTUNATELY, THE FOLLOWING day we discovered that nobody was in those cars. I later found out that vehicle manufacturers' design of alarm systems contributed to the confusion. We surmised that the sensitivity switches interpreted the rocking of the cars from the hurricane force winds or the wave action from the flood water to be an attempt to steal the car. In our case not all vehicles had this feature. The dispersed pattern of parked cars flashing their lights added to the realism that people were inside. I almost committed half of my team to a suicide mission to rescue imaginary people from empty cars in a hostile environment. Sometimes I would rather the repercussions of my decisions be lucky rather than good.

The last firefighter to join our team was late and almost didn't make it at all. Tom Kennedy is a young Irish immigrant who married a medical professional. To many of us, Tom's Irish brogue was a reminder of our ancestral roots. He was a dedicated volunteer who in the past held an officer rank and was currently serving as a motor pump operator and chauffeur for our trucks. He often provided instruction to the new probationary firefighters at our training drills. Probies were new recruits and usually spent their first year learning the art of firefighting. He was an outstanding instructor and easily imparted his knowledge to the new guys. His service in our fire department was a welcome distraction from his more mundane career in the financial world. Like many volunteers, his job put the bread and butter on his family's table, but being a firefighter added more purpose and excitement into his life. Whenever he was in the firehouse, he was always accompanied by his two sons who probably knew more about the firehouse than some of our more seasoned members. They prided themselves as being junior firefighters and looked forward to the day they would be officially sworn in as probies.

Tom spent the day of Superstorm Sandy's arrival finding a safe place to evacuate his wife and three kids. He returned to his home in late afternoon and secured valuable property inside and loose items outside. Satisfied, Tom started his journey to the firehouse in a kayak. Along the way he met his neighbors, Mike and Judy Scotko with their son Michael, and their dog. Michael was also a firefighter with the PBFD. Seeing them struggling in the flood waters, Tom Kennedy gave them his kayak.

This was right about the time of Sandy's initial assault. At 8:50 pm an ocean buoy fifteen miles southeast of Breezy Point recorded a wave of 32.5 feet. This wave carried with it death and destruction on its crest and was now crashing over Breezy Point with Tom in its crosshairs. Only his inner strength and determination would overcome what happened next. Tom was in an open and unprotected area when white capped waves began rapidly crossing our neighborhood, uniting the Atlantic Ocean with waters of the Jamaica Bay on the northern side of the property. He was immediately engulfed by the turbulent waters and tossed about, mercilessly bombarded by waves and loose debris. Thanks to his experience as a swimmer and the grace of God, he narrowly avoided being drowned. Battered and exhausted, he limped into the clubhouse.

One of the firefighters was gravely concerned with his condition and asked me to check on him. I found him on the floor shivering violently but with the floodwaters rising inside the clubhouse he was going to have to move. Tom was soaked to the bone and looked like he was in the battle of his life. We got him some dry clothes and treated him to prevent hypothermia. As a volunteer he had a choice to stay at home and protect his property but he made the courageous decision to join his brother firefighters and risked his life to save others. After a time, Tom was able to recover from his ordeal and with renewed strength, he joined us and was a highly welcome addition. This night would be a night of continuous heavy work. In the hundred plus years of our department's history, this would be the most difficult event ever experienced. I was elated that Tom and the other firefighters made the Herculean effort to save lives.

In a short time, the water outside the clubhouse was at eight feet above the street level and inside we could see the water bubbling up through the tile seams on the floor. We already had at least three feet inside the clubhouse and the water continued to rise. The clubhouse quickly became a public shelter as soaked and weary people slowly gravitated there for sanctuary.

There was one elderly lady who was soaked and looked like she was suffering from the early effects of hypothermia, so I helped her out of the frigid October water and carried her to the stage. The interior of the clubhouse was dark and flooded by the surge. The scattered light from our flashlights reflected across the water and floating debris. I was wearing my department issued bunker gear and wrapped her up in my heavy-duty fire coat. Unfortunately, we were separated during the night and I never saw the coat again. I would wind up fighting the biggest fire in my life in just my bunker pants and sweatshirt.

Mike, Judy and their dog safely made it to the clubhouse in Tom's kayak. Inside they remember the experience to be solemn, even somber, with scattered debris floating in the standing water. He said, "It's great to see the community sticking together and helping each other. The cell phone lines were jammed and I was concerned for the well-being of our adult daughter. It was an awful night."

Around the same time, two light rescue boats from the Rockaway Point Fire Department (RPFD) arrived at the clubhouse. They courageously made multiple trips in the raging water to rescue people who were trying to get to the clubhouse. In a short while our numbers had increased to forty evacuees and at least twenty firefighters. Many people feared that the flood water would continue to rise and that we would drown in the building. This prompted our first discussion about evacuation. One of our evacuees lived in a two-story home across from the clubhouse on Point Breeze Avenue. He offered his house as an alternative but the problem was how to cross the raging flood waters, which now deluged Point Breeze Avenue. My reluctance to move people in the middle of a hurricane came from past military experience, where troop movements even under the best of circumstances could easily result in some injuries. We broke into storage closets and inventoried all of the items in hopes of finding some long piece of rope that we could use as a lifeline to cross the raging water. The best we could find were two sets of skimpy Christmas lights that would barely cover the distance. Our plans to evacuate were dashed when we realized that the house we were going to commandeer may have already been damaged. The risk was too high that the house was no longer secure on its foundation and could topple after sixty people found their way to the second floor.

In disasters of this proportion, no one really knows how bad it's going to get, how high the water will rise and what other hazards will come into play. During a disaster it is the "unknown" that can paralyze one with fear. It's easy to quarterback on the next day when the event is over and the true damages are known. Although many emergency response organizations have prepared instruction manuals on how to handle disasters, the play book on how to manage in a disaster with unknown variables does not exist. After listening to the input from my officers, I announced that we were staying in the clubhouse and that the evacuees would be placed on the stage that was four feet above the floor and only one foot above the water. I knew we were running out of options and needed help, so I asked the entire group to gather together. I gave them an update on our situation and an honest appraisal of our limited options. At the end of this impromptu briefing I said, "You might think this unusual but I think it's appropriate- -please join me in praying the "Our Father." It was a simple gesture, similar to a coach of an athletic team huddling his athletes to say a prayer in hopes that the Almighty would help the team to play at their very best. Our team desperately needed a win. We did a total of three "prayer huddles." The first two were "Our Fathers" and the last one was a "Hail Mary" and after each prayer I saw a positive change that told me someone was listening, and in my opinion these positive changes could be considered miracles.

After our first prayer, the RPFD Boat Rescue Crew came to the clubhouse. When their weary bodies climbed through the window in their wetsuits, I asked if they were here to rescue us or if we were here to rescue them? The boat rescue option gave us an additional capability. The fury of the storm, combined with the flood waters, convinced many people to abandon their homes and seek safer sanctuary. The rescue boat would prove to be a valuable option for rescue.

Sometime during the night, we experienced an electrical failure and the entire community went dark. Our flashlights helped but they would only be good for as long as the batteries lasted, and we knew we had a long night ahead of us. The darkness was interrupted when we spotted the orange glow of a house fire about a half mile away. Despite the water being twelve feet deep, the winds were spreading the fire. Here we were trapped inside the clubhouse with our abandoned firehouse totally flooded and our two fire trucks were completely submerged. We were receiving scattered reports from texts and social media that some people were trapped in their attics with the water still rising and the members wanted to go on their own and attempt to rescue their stranded neighbors. I needed to keep the team together before this turned into a mutiny. The storm was raging and it was too dangerous to commit our resources at that time. We would probably not have been successful and would unnecessarily risk our lives. I needed to keep the department together and save our resources for the right time.

Some of the firefighters came to me and asked, "When are we going to fight the fire, Chief?" We were now managing a public shelter with forty people in our care. We couldn't abandon them and leave them on their own. As firefighters our first priority is to protect life and then protect property. By the time the third person asked me the same question I became testy and repeated sternly, "We will fight the fire at the right time and not a moment sooner or a moment later!" The truth was no one had a crystal ball that would tell them when the right moment was. Quietly, I said a prayer to Saint Anthony to help me determine the right time to move out. He was the patron saint of seekers of lost articles. I needed his help to find the right time to make a critical move. I needed a sign, and when the time was right, Saint Anthony responded.

In the meantime, I needed more information to develop a proper plan. Primarily, I needed to know how deep the water could get yet still allow us to operate our trucks. It was doubtful the trucks would start after being flooded, but if they did, how deep could they operate without seizing the engine? The engine within a fire truck needs air to breathe and a clear path for the exhaust to be discharged. If the water blocked the intakes near the carburetor or the exhaust pipe the truck would die. Then there was the question of manpower. Breezy Point is a community with many police officers and firefighters, but most of the city's First Responders were called in for overtime to protect the city during the hurricane. I started to inventory the skills of the forty survivors and was lucky to find a retired firefighter from the Fire Department of New York (FDNY). Not only was he a firefighter but at one time in his career he was a chauffeur on a FDNY engine truck. I gathered our chauffeurs and together we began to pick his brain on the operation of fire trucks in flood waters. We estimated the depth of the water outside to be 12-15 feet deep. We felt comfortable that the engine sat up high enough to operate in five to six feet of water, but our limiting factor was the exhaust system. The exhaust pipe sat low and after much discussion I felt we would be lucky to handle four to five feet of water. Later, when the department ordered a new truck, we would get one with an exhaust stack like a snorkel and discharge its exhaust gases well above the cab.

Meanwhile, the wind-driven fire was spreading quickly and the flood waters gave no indication of subsiding. The fire quickly spread to forty homes. Angry red flames danced and licked the night sky fifty feet in the air. Thick black smoke laden with red glowing softball-sized embers blanketed the area, raining destruction in its path. There were over two thousand homes downwind of the fire and we stood to lose the entire community. We needed another divine intervention. We huddled together and said our second "Our Father."

The flood waters came in four hours earlier than the scheduled moon high tide. It was scheduled for 9:10 pm. If the tide didn't start to recede for another four hours we were probably doomed. Only if the flood receded earlier than expected could we gain the mobility to continue to rescue people and fight the fire. The clubhouse was made of concrete block and I used the mortar lines as an indicator of the high-water mark inside the building. On the northeast corner of the building there was a stop sign that acted as an outside high-water mark. At about 9:15 pm I noticed a slight change on my interior high-water gauge. It was almost imperceptible but it looked like it was receding. I quickly went to the outside gauge and despite wind-driven wave action I confirmed that the tide was going out. We now had our second miracle.

We were fortunate to have three highly dedicated volunteer fire departments in our community. Although we frequently competed against each other, and there was often friendly competition, we knew we could count on the Roxbury and Rockaway Fire Departments to work together with us. Earlier in the day, we learned that the Fire Department of New York (FDNY) removed all of their fire apparatus and firefighters from the entire Rockaway Peninsula in advance of the storm, so it was up to us. We were never directly informed of this decision. It was through back-channel communications that we learned of the plan. We had many former members join the FDNY who were now FDNY firefighters or dispatchers and the word was passed. It was a decision that was made to protect their people and equipment. We'd always worked in unison with them and had a successful partnership. We now felt suddenly alone and knew that it was up to us to get the job done. However, we also knew that the FDNY would return at the earliest possible moment. After witnessing firsthand the fury of Hurricane Sandy and the resulting devastation, deep down I seriously doubted they would be able to return to the peninsula and join the battle.

When I first became chief, I noticed that several of our members routinely used strong language in expressing themselves. The fellas often let loose with curses. They did it so frequently, I thought that they suffered from Tourette's syndrome. I made it clear that it didn't reflect well on the department when foul language was used. However, I did concede there may be rare occasions when foul language would be appropriate. Up until that evening no one ever heard me curse, but we were trapped in the clubhouse by the tidal surge of Hurricane Sandy and my frustration was overwhelming as I monitored the expanding fire. I used my gloved hand to punch the concrete-block wall and I vividly recall saying, "This is bad; this is really bad; this is real fucking bad." I turned to see one of my firefighters, Mike Scotko, right over my shoulder. He was one of our younger firefighters and up until that time he'd never heard me curse. His eyes were as wide as a manhole cover. I turned to him and said, "In the military, I experienced some nasty and fucked up situations. This is the most fucked up situation I have ever experienced." His eyes opened even wider and his shock was readily apparent. I didn't know if his shock came more from my uncharacteristic use of curse words, or because he now knew the gravity of the situation.

At around 10:00 pm, I noticed the wind changed direction from the northeast to the southeast. As a pilot I knew this was a sign that we were now in the back end of the storm. I rallied the people together to tell them the good news and that the worst of the storm was now behind us. The wind change combined with the knowledge that the flood waters were receding gave us all hope that our situation was improving. Since we were all together, we did another "prayer huddle." This time I was called away to settle a dispute so I asked one of our seasoned firefighters, Steve Glavey, to lead us in prayer. This time he said the "Hail Mary," and while the "Our Father" had worked twice already, this prayer would help us to pull off the most important miracle of the night.

One downside of the wind direction shifting, was that the clubhouse was now directly downwind from the inferno. The smoke plume carrying the ashes and fiery embers was now aimed directly at us. Black smoke infiltrated our building, burning our eyes and causing us to choke. We secured windows to prevent the smoke from entering the building but all efforts failed. Next, we attempted to ventilate the building but again our efforts failed. By now, not only did we have difficulty seeing each other, we were having problems breathing. Smoke and debris from over 100 homes blanketed our position and rained fiery embers upon us.

It was now that former Chief Kurt Bruder came up to me and said that we had to evacuate. He was right. The clubhouse had a wood roof covered by shingles. All night the shingles were being blown away. Now that we were inside the smoke plume, we were experiencing the effects of a firestorm of epic portions that threatened everything in its path. The night sky was filled with fiery embers that made it look like the air was on fire. The embers would sizzle and explode as they hit the water. It wouldn't take much to start the roof on fire or to cause the fire to jump behind us.

Listening is a key element of leadership. I called the firefighters together to discuss our predicament and to develop a plan of action. I was surrounded by some intelligent people and needed their input to develop a plan that would work. We reviewed our options and realized that we didn't have many. We had to get our evacuees to safety and then find a way to fight this monster fire until the FDNY

11

came back to the peninsula. We couldn't stay where we were and we couldn't brave the elements on our own. I called for the firemen qualified to drive the fire trucks to overcome the obstacles between the two buildings, find their way back to our firehouse and see if they could start the trucks. There were wind-driven waves blocking their way between the two buildings. I held out little hope that the rigs would start after being under five feet of water. It was a risky but necessary decision in that we had to determine the availability of the trucks as an option. We had to see if the trucks were operable. There really seemed to be no other option.

With those volunteers dispatched I was huddled with some of the firefighters assessing our situation when I heard the engines on our two trucks roar to life. There was no reason why they should have started after being under five feet of water. Right then we knew we had our third miracle and that the "Hail Mary" worked. I also knew that my quiet prayer to Saint Anthony, asking for information about the right time to deploy was answered. If the water was four to five feet deep it would be the right time to deploy.

Our plan was to create a human lifeline of firefighters, escort the forty plus survivors and their pets to the firehouse, and evacuate them to safety on our trucks. Saint Thomas More Church was the next available public shelter. It was approximately a half mile away and upwind of the firestorm. It would take several trips and it was doubtful that the trucks would last, but at least we would get some of the civilians to safety. Thankfully, the standing water was four to five feet deep so I gave the order to move out.

The difference between being a paid city firefighter and a volunteer firefighter is that we as volunteers lived in the community that we guarded. We had the same responsibility to protect lives and property but unlike our FDNY brothers and sisters, most of the people in our jurisdiction were friends, relatives, or a neighbor–and we all knew them on a first name basis. All of the buildings and homes in our community were well known to each of us and carried with them special memories.

As we left the clubhouse to start the human lifeline to rescue our evacuees, I looked back at the building we just left and a kaleidoscope of memories cascaded through my brain. As a youngster I would go there to watch movies on rainy days. I attended teen dances there and danced for the first time with my teenage sweetheart. The clubhouse was the place where my farewell party was held the day before I joined the Air Force and it was also later the place where I gave a speech to the community association in hopes of being elected to the board of directors.

We made small talk with the survivors in order to relax them as they made their way down our human chain of firemen. With the power outage and the blinding black plume of smoke and all the events that happened so far, I knew that this was the darkest moment in the history of the PBFD. I also knew that if we could continue to act as a team and get help from outside sources, we could succeed and turn this entire experience into our finest hour. As I turned away from the clubhouse, I had a sick feeling in my stomach that this may be the last time I saw this building standing—that it would all be rubble.

Debris and erosion made the roads unsafe and when the trucks moved, they pushed a two-foot bow wave of water in front of them. Again, there was no mechanical explanation why the trucks continued to function. Each truck made three round trips. I believed a good leader looks out for his people and I was the last person to leave the firehouse.

I was lucky to have a small team of dedicated firefighters but none of us had ever fought a fire of this magnitude. My team included: two high school students, two college students, a stock broker, an editor of the local newspaper, a corporate human resources specialist, a truck driver from a well-known package delivery company, a member of Local 30, and four off-duty police officers. Two of the off-duty policemen were brothers and earlier that evening their father, who was a retired law enforcement officer asked if his membership in the PBFD could be re-activated. He knew this night had the potential to be dangerous and he wanted to be with them. He and I joined the

13

department as teenagers and I happily re-activated him. I needed every able-bodied person with firefighting experience and a cool head under pressure. The last person on the team was me, a retired Air Force Rescue pilot and a retired FAA Aviation Safety Manager. As a trained Air Force pilot, I received many hours of emergency training. This helped me to stay calm and think logically even if the aircraft was coming apart around me. In the event of an in-flight emergency, we were trained to restore order, overcome chaos and bring the aircraft to a safe landing. Now the challenge was to stay calm and think logically as the neighborhood was coming apart around us. The mission was essentially the same: we would also restore order, overcome chaos and help keep the neighborhood safe. Together we would do our best to prevent anyone from dying and do our best to preserve the homes and memories of the members of our community. The fire, however, was continuing to spread to well over a hundred homes. At best, once we were on-scene we would be lucky to contain the expansion. We desperately needed the FDNY.

On the Brooklyn side of the Marine Parkway Bridge, across from Breezy Point, hundreds of FDNY firefighters were preparing to join the fight. They could see the massive inferno gutting our neighborhood — for some of them it could be their own homes. They were eager to get into the fight but the storm held them back. Seething with frustration they waited. It would be up to the "vollies" to hold back the fires until help arrived, if they were still alive.

CHAPTER 2

Growing up in Breezy Point

I GREW UP in Breezy Point, New York during the fifties and sixties. Breezy Point is part of the Borough of Queens and City of New York. It is surrounded on three sides by the Atlantic Ocean and Jamaica Bay on the western tip of the Rockaway Peninsula. On a straight line it is only fifteen miles from Times Square but it is worlds apart from that glitter and glamor. The person who named the place got it right: there was always a breeze coming off the ocean. This breeze typically lowered the temperature by ten degrees and in the summers, before air conditioning became popular, the breezes were a blessing. But during the winters the unrestricted winds blowing off the ocean carried

15

a sting and force that made it difficult to venture outdoors. For those who did go outside, the weather only served to make them tough.

Breezy Point is primarily a summer community. Some parts of the neighborhood started out as tents built on platforms. Later, more permanent structures like bungalows were built. They were inexpensive and very close together. Because of the low cost of a house the neighborhood became a "middle class mecca." Though there were over 2800 homes in the community, only one hundred families were pioneers and chose to live there year-round. My family was one of them. As a cost savings measure the street lights were turned off during the off season and the all-year-round homes had special water lines that were operational twelve months of the year. If only the power was off when Sandy visited, we would have averted community-wide fires.

The sidewalks were crowded from Memorial Day to Labor Day and bicycles were banned during that time period. There were only two exemptions to the banned bicycle rule: the local parish priest who on occasion had to administer last rites and the local liquor store was allowed home delivery. If one ever saw both bikes parked outside a house, you knew there was a problem.

The summer would abruptly start on Memorial Day and end on Labor Day. Labor Day was a sad time for some of the permanent residents because most of our friends left to go back to their winter homes and we wouldn't see them again till the next May. Our friendships would be suspended until the next summer season and budding summer romances would be placed on hold.

Breezy Point in the summer is an idyllic place. The weather and ocean are at their best and complement each other. The long hot and sunny days combine with the warm sandy beaches and invigorating surf are the best. The evenings are cool and there is an ever-present sound of waves gently breaking on the shore. Contributing to the relaxed environment, sounds such as a bell buoy making its ringing sound after being rocked by waves from Jamaica Bay combined with the ever-frequent squawks from local sea gulls and the crisp salt air.

Most people are on vacation and full of smiles. Recreation pursuits include swimming, basketball, baseball and surfing. It is a special place for a young teenager who is now beyond the stage of thinking the opposite sex is full of germs. Instead, their brain starts to send messages alerting them to the attractiveness of the opposite sex. Physically they are approaching their prime. Emotionally everything is new and intense. Casual friendships easily turn into romantic relationships that create memories lasting for a lifetime. Many summer romances lead to more permanent states such as marriage while others evaporate. In both situations the experiences are highly valued and rarely forgotten.

Like many other special places, Breezy Point in the summer becomes a launching pad. Each year a new group of teenagers' step onto this stage and become actors in a drama of awakening emotions. As they get older and begin their life's journey throughout the world, they store their happy memories in a special place with hopes of someday returning to re-capture the magic. If anything should adversely happen to the center of their favorite memories, they return to fiercely protect that special place. That's what happened after Superstorm Sandy nearly destroyed the community. They came from all over to help rebuild the place that held so many special memories.

In the off season, I focused mainly on my studies and my swimming. I had a few friends who also lived in Breezy all year round. We were very close and found a variety of ways to pass the time. Touch football in the sand was always a favorite and we were also highly influenced by the TV shows which mostly portrayed military actions from WWII. I was born five years after WWII ended. We were the offspring of war-weary veterans who were making up for lost time. By the time we were ten years old there were popular TV shows like the *Rat Patrol, Victory at Sea* and *Combat*. Movies like *The Longest Day* and *The Great Escape* were also popular. My friends and I picked out a steep sand dune on the bayside and we played a game called "Soldier." On the surface it appeared as if we were imitating some of the actors and pretending that we were charging an imaginary

17

machine gun nest or we were trying to escape some invisible artillery fire. But some of us were re-enacting the stories told us by our relatives who were combat veterans. We took turns running down the hill, dodging the imaginary enemy bullets and eventually coming to rest after some dramatic fall and a flurry of sand. After a short moment of silence, we would magically come back to life, shake off the sand and climb the hill to wait our next turn.

The "Ops Tempo" on the sand dune would increase dramatically whenever a couple of the local year-round young ladies would show up to observe our imaginary battles. Our parents did their best to create an age of innocence for us, but the TV stories from WWII actually were forecasters of what my generation was to experience. In the late sixties, these same sand dunes were the place where my friends and I held farewell beach parties for those who were being drafted or joining the armed forces during the Vietnam War. We sang folk songs and drank adult beverages and sent our friends to another world, hoping that they would return safely. After the attacks of 9/11 our community built a monument at the same location to the thirty plus people from Breezy who were murdered in the World Trade Center.

The neighborhood was predominantly Irish-American and each household had from four to seven kids on the average. In the early fifties, the median annual income of the public servants ranged from $3,000 to $6,000 and placed most of us very close to the poverty line, but if we were poor, we didn't know it. Nearly everyone was happy. We had a roof over our heads and consumed three meals a day. And for the adults there was always beer in the fridge. I had three older brothers and a younger sister. Later the social scientists would refer to my generation as the baby boomers. In the sixties my friends and I were the teenage offspring of the "Greatest Generation." They witnessed the Great Depression and the Second World War. When they returned from the war many of them traded their military uniforms for police and firefighters' uniforms.

Breezy is a generational community. My grandparents first owned the bungalow in the early 1930s. My mother, her three sisters and her brother grew up in the house and enjoyed their summers there. In the early fifties, my parents inherited the home. Breezy is also a faith-based community, predominantly Roman Catholic. There are three Catholic churches and two non-denominational Christian Churches in the neighborhood. On Sundays in the summer, each Catholic Church had a Mass every hour starting at 7:00 am and ending with the last Mass at noon. The churches were packed. In six hours, nearly all of the community filtered through the churches. If you skipped church many people wanted to know why. We all worried about each other's chances at eternal salvation. The priest who gave the shortest sermon was the one who was most loved. The churches were not air-conditioned and the services after ten o'clock were unbearable. Usually, the parishioner who stayed out the latest on Saturday night suffered the most through the later Masses.

When the homes started to heat up with the morning sun, we all escaped to the beaches on the bay or the ocean. As youngsters we mostly went to the bay. The water was calmer and it was a great place to learn how to swim. As my swimming abilities increased, the water became my friend. We had community-sponsored swim races and we competed against each other.

As I became more confident, I picked up a mask and snorkel and taught myself how to dive. I discovered a new dimension to my neighborhood. At high tide, the visibility was excellent and I observed the variety of marine life that lived near the shore. I knew that the por-gies and black fish liked to feed in the areas near the pilings of the piers and the crabs liked to hide on the inside of an abandoned tire. Several years later I got a spear with a rubber sling and hunted some of these fish for dinner. Every hour a ferry boat from Sheepshead Bay, Brooklyn would arrive at our dock. The passengers on the weekend were mostly Brooklyn residents who were looking for an escape from the heat. As the boat approached the pier, a bunch of my friends would grab our masks, fins and snorkels and swim toward the ar-riving vessel. In a nasal tone, due to our masks covering our nos-es, we would shout out "Coins-Coins-Coins" and the passengers on the upper deck would reach into their pockets for spare change and throw the coins into the water. As a group, we would dive after the coins in water nearly twelve feet deep with the hopes of recovering the money. Usually, the one who could swim the fastest and be able to hold his breath the longest went home with the greatest number of coins. In between dives, we stored the coins in our face masks and it was easy to see who was having a good day. Later that money would be spent at the local candy store.

As time went on, we developed a greater awareness of the opposite sex. The girls in our crowd usually were on the dock observing the battles that were taking place in the attempt to recover treasure discarded by the tourists. The battles became intensified in that not only did we want the money but we also wanted to gain the attention of some young girl on the dock.

When my swimming abilities were strong enough, I went to the ocean beach on the southern side of the peninsula and learned how to ride the waves. At first the white water and foam from the crushing waves scared me but as I became used to this experience, I learned how to use the energy in the cresting wave to carry me to the sandy shoreline. I then learned how to swim past the breaking waves and I began to study the approaching rollers to determine if I could ride them. I studied how the older kids body surfed and mimicked their actions and it wasn't long before I could feel the pull of the approaching wave and instinctively knew which wave was worthy of riding. It was a euphoric feeling to be rocketed down the face of a wave. For a young kid the sense of acceleration and speed was exhilarating. We had contests to see who could ride the wave to the shallowest point. The varying weather conditions helped to bring bigger waves. A tropical storm system sitting off the coast of Virginia would bring the New York City coastline some of the best surf. As we built our strength and confidence, we became willing to surf the bigger waves. The ocean became our friend and constantly provided us with comfort and entertainment. We usually spent the entire day body surfing and later as teenagers we transferred this skill into riding surfboards.

The clubhouse operated by the Point Breeze Association became the center for our social interactions. Rainy summer days in Breezy were the worst and being stuck in a small bungalow with a multitude of siblings was a formula for disaster. Fortunately, during those dreary days, the clubhouse would open up and show movies. The clubhouse was also used for public meetings and for one week in the summer a bazaar was held as a fund raiser by the local volunteer fire department. The vollies had small tents on the lawn and the shelves were lined with toys and games. There was a spinning wheel with numbers and a corresponding mat with matching numbers. The lucky person who placed a bet on a winning number walked away with a prize. The area was lighted with strings of lights similar to what one would see at a country fair. We even had a cotton candy machine. Of course, the only person who made real money was the purveyor of the prizes.

As young adolescents we returned to the clubhouse for our Tuesday night teen dances. It was a rite of passage for many of us and the beginning of the socialization process. The same girls that we grew up with and tried to impress with our coin diving and surfing skills were now all dressed up, waiting for us to build up the courage and ask them to dance. In the beginning it was easier to surf a ten-foot wave than to ask someone to dance and risk being rejected. The lights were dimmed and on the stage was a local rock band playing our favorite sounds. Our dances included the "Twist," "the Swim," "the Monkey," "the Mashed Potato" the "Cha-Cha" and the "Freddie." The guy who could best demonstrate his dancing abilities was the guy least likely to be rejected, but for me the best dance was a slow dance. Typically, our parents could be seen in the shadows outside of the clubhouse looking inside to see if we were leaving enough room for the Holy Ghost (Spirit). Usually, the last dance of the night was a slow one and it had special meaning. If a guy was lucky, he might be able to walk the young lady home holding hands with the hopes of a good night kiss.

Our crowd lived by the music of our generation. In the daytime, we listened on tiny transistor radios to the surfing music of the Beach Boys and at night to the Beatles and others. It was as if the music was written for us and we lived every moment of it.

When our crowd gathered for either the teen dance or for a beach party, we would number over a hundred kids. We were within one or two years of age of each other and it was understood that we had to stay clear of the social groups of our older siblings. If I discovered one of my older brothers engaged in some of the more advanced forms of socialization such as kissing or making out, I would have an advantage at the dinner table. It was always the younger sibling who gave up the older ones to curry favor with the parents. Of course, any joy that would be had was short-lived, and it would usually result in some fists being thrown. Irish-American brothers could be tough on each other.

During the winter months, I had full run of the beach. I had a bicycle and knew every inch of the neighborhood. In the winter the sand would freeze and I was able to use my bike to explore the sand dunes and the isolated areas. Some of my neighbors were fishermen and had their secret spots. The fishermen did not want to disclose their favorite fishing

spot. When the catch was good, they would drop off the extra fish at our house. In my travels I came across my neighbor fishing at his favorite secret spot and he already had a good catch. Although fishermen are not normally talkative, I struck up a conversation with him. I asked him many questions about how to fish. The unspoken understanding was that he would share his knowledge of his sport as long as I didn't give up his favorite fishing locations. He explained to me how the fish run, the meaning of the different colors of the water and how the changing tides affected how the fish would feed. He told me that it was important to study the movement of the birds. The sea gulls would tell you the location of the fish and more importantly, they could tell you if the weather was going to turn bad. He said if you see the birds leaving the ocean shoreline for the bay on the north side of the neighborhood the weather was going to get rough. If the sea gulls keep going to the other side of the bay near Brooklyn, we were in for a hell of a storm. Little did I know that this tidbit of information from the kind fisherman would be of critical use to me some fifty years later.

But, as I said, Breezy Point was primarily a summer colony. We lived in bungalows that were designed to be comfortable in the heat of the summer. No one had the luxury of an air conditioner. The houses were small and had many windows that allowed for the cool air to enter. Each window had a screen that was effective in keeping out the mosquitoes, flies and other insects. The interior walls (with the exception of the bathroom) only went three quarters of the way to the ceiling and the bedroom doorways were only equipped with curtains. This allowed for easy air flow during the hot and humid summer nights. It also allowed for just about any conversation to be heard in every room. There were no secrets, as the walls in the crowded households literally had ears. Each bedroom had a set of bunk beds that acted as sleep lockers and helped to optimize any available space.

On the average, the bungalows were only 740 square feet and were made of wood. The houses were built close together. It would be easy to hear your neighbor's on-going conversations and occasional argument. If neighboring homes were each equipped with a telephone, members of both families would scramble to answer the phone when either phone rang. Initially, there were only party lines. For those without telephones there was a building that held a bank of phone booths providing a simple form of communication. Normally, this close-quarters living with its lack of privacy posed a problem to most people, but here it was simply part of the way we lived. Breezy Point existed within the shadows of the Manhattan skyline and its residents came from other congested areas within the city. They were used to this style of living. Besides, the transparent communications led to a sense of closeness and created family friendships that have been handed down from generation to generation.

My father was a New York City Police Officer and on many nights his firefighter and police friends would drop by for a visit. Beer was the choice beverage and it served a dual purpose. It quenched the thirst from a summer day and it also helped dull the senses after a difficult day. The pop top was not invented yet and the only way to open a beer was with a can opener. The can opener was affectionately called a church key. How it got this sacrilegious nickname I will never know, but it stuck. At the end of each story, I could hear the "Church Key" being used to crack open fresh cans in preparation of the next story.

It was at night in bed that I first heard their stories about helping people in distress. The curtains and walls that only went three quarters of the way to the ceiling allowed me to listen in to their conversations. I heard the story of how my father in his rookie first year prevented a crazed horse strapped to a wagon from running into a crowd of pedestrians near Times Square, and another about the time he disarmed a robber in a Manhattan restaurant without having to use his gun. He would later be inducted into the NYPD's Honor Legion for that act. I would hear about firefighters entering smoke-laden burning buildings with the hopes of finding survivors. Today's technology of Self-Contained Breathing Apparatus (SCBA) did not exist in those days, so, my Dad's friends would walk into a burning building equipped with only an axe, a pike pole, a charged line, a spotlight, a strong set of lungs and whatever courage they had inside. I would drift off to sleep halfway through their stories and turn their words over in my dreams.

Later, I would come to refer to these people as Guardians, those souls who put their lives on the line for the well-being of others. From a very young age I only had one desire in my life. It was to become one of them.

CHAPTER 3

Fighters of a Never-Ending War

THE FIREFIGHTER'S CREED

I am proud to be a firefighter.
I revere that long line of expert firefighters who
by their devotion to duty and sacrifice of self,
have made it possible for me to be a member of a

service honored and respected, in good times and
bad, throughout the world.
I never, by word or deed, will bring reproach upon
the fair name of the fire service, nor permit others
to do so unchallenged.
I will cheerfully and willingly obey all lawful
orders.
I will always be on time to relieve,
and shall endeavor to do more,
rather than less, than my share.
I will always be at my station,
alert and attending to my duties.
I shall, so far as I am able,
bring to my Seniors solutions, not problems.
I shall live joyously,
but always with due regard for the rights and
privileges of others.
I shall endeavor to be a model citizen in the
community in which I live.
I shall sell my life dearly to my enemy fire but give
it freely to rescue those in peril.
With God's help,
I shall endeavor to be one of His noblest Works.

EVER SINCE MANKIND discovered fire, it has been fighting a never-ending war against it. The discovery of the controlled use of fire was one of mankind's first great innovations, but with it came a heavy responsibility. It needed to discover ways to control it, extinguish it, train personnel and develop new equipment and procedures to manage it. Over the years, the fire battles both increased and intensified. Several major cities were destroyed.

The history of firefighting began in ancient Rome by Marcus Licinus Crassus, a wealthy Roman general. Fires in Rome were common and caused major damage. He created the first Roman brigade of 500 firefighters, called "Cohortes Vigiles" or "Watchmen of the City."

At the first cries for help, these firefighters would arrive on scene, and Crassus would then negotiate the cost of their services with the property owner. If the negotiations failed the building would burn to the ground.

In September, 1666, the Great Fire of London nearly destroyed the entire city. In the aftermath, changes were made that contributed greatly to organized firefighting. The first fire insurance company called the Fire Office, was established in 1667. Other similar companies soon followed. Policyholders were given a badge or fire mark to attach to their building so that it could be identified in case of a fire. The fire companies worked for the insurance companies to help lower the cost of claims.

In New Amsterdam, Governor Peter Stuyvesant established the first fire ordinance in the Dutch Colony. The act required that all funds received from fines levied for dirty chimneys should be used for the maintenance of buckets, hooks and ladders. The first fire company was organized in 1657 and was equipped with 250 leather buckets made by a New Amsterdam shoemaker.

Benjamin Franklin was a volunteer firefighter and in 1736 he helped to create the first fire department in Philadelphia. George Washington, the future president, was a volunteer firefighter in Alexandria, Virginia. In 1774, as a member of the Friendship Veterans Fire Engine Company, he bought a new fire engine and gave it to the town.

In 1737, the General Assembly of the Colony in New York City passed an act which established the Volunteer Fire Department of the City of New York which operated under this name for 128 years. The dedicated and heroic service of the Volunteer Fire Department (VFD) protected the lives and property of the citizens of the city until superseded by the paid Metropolitan Fire Department (MPD) after the close of the Civil War in 1865.

The change from volunteer companies to paid firefighters was necessary to meet the needs of the expanding city. Also, the fire equipment was becoming more sophisticated and expensive. The VFD survived financially by being subsidized by the fire insurance companies. Competition for insurance payments from the independent VFDs was fierce and frequently resulted in bitter brawls and feuds between companies. These combined factors helped to lead to the abolishment of the VFD system.

In 1870, the Tweed Charter replaced the Metropolitan Fire Department with the Fire Department of the City of New York. The primary visible change was the re-lettering of the apparatus from MFD to FDNY. In 1898, the boroughs of Richmond and Queens consolidated with New York City and made the transition to full time paid status from volunteer non-paid.

In the early 1900s twelve beachfront summer communities within New York City started up volunteer companies. This was done to augment the summer coverage and because the communities had mostly wooden bungalow structures built very close together. The city allocated firehouses and companies based upon density of residential communities. Most beachfront communities were only populated during the summer months and as a result had limited full time fire coverage. These volunteer fire companies created the Volunteer Fire Association of New York City. They were highly trained and had reliable fire equipment. Financially, they relied upon community donations and other fund-raising events. They also, on occasion, received funds from state and federal grants. The firefighters were non-paid volunteers who worked well with their full time paid FDNY counterparts. Because of the nature of the fire service, both groups were referred to as being "professional." The local volunteer firefighters were the first to be on-scene. Upon arrival, the FDNY assumed the role of incident commander and were in charge of the operation.

Firefighters are warriors in a war that never ends. While the battles don't occur every day, these "Fire Warriors" and their equipment stand ready at all times. When the battles do occur, they welcome the opportunity to do their best to triumph. The fire battles can be one of the fiercest forms of combat.

In 1966, at the young age of sixteen, I joined the Point Breeze Fire Department. I didn't know anything about the history of the fire service nor the fact that I was becoming a small cog in the global wheel of the never-ending war to fight fire. I did know that my three older brothers were members of the PBFD, and the community needed every able-bodied person to be a part of the organization. Like the other two volunteer fire departments in Roxbury and Rockaway Point most new recruits were making the transition from being a lifeguard to a firefighter. The three volunteer departments were pillars of strength in the neighborhood. The training we received prepared us not only for our current duties, but in future careers in the fire service, law enforcement and in my case the Air Rescue Service of the United States Air Force. The training environment of a volunteer fire department acts as a leadership incubator that helps spawn future leaders and professionals. The most important day for any firefighter is the day they stand up to take the oath to become a firefighter. It is a day that a person makes a commitment to put the lives of others ahead of their own. Some say it is the only day that we are true heroes. The other days we are just doing our job.

The training to become a firefighter was intense. It was given by senior members who were mostly former FDNY firefighters. At this young age it was easy to drag hoses, climb ladders and carry victims to safety. We listened attentively to our mentors and instructors.

Our department had a fine history that started in 1910, and stories would abound in the back room about big fires and how they managed to put them out. On the average we received 120 calls a year and of course none of us wanted to miss a "Big One."

One example of a big event is the story of the "Golden Venture" in 1993. The Golden Venture was a cargo ship that became stranded on a sandbar off Breezy Point, and it was carrying 300 undocumented immigrants from China who jumped overboard when the ship ran aground about 300 yards off Fort Tilden. My brother John was on the first truck that responded and it was national news at the time. Unfortunately, ten of the passengers died as a result of drowning after jumping off the side of the ship into the raging surf.

In Breezy, a fire was very dangerous because if one house caught fire, the strong winds from the ocean could cause it to spread rapidly. Our training focused on knocking the fire down quickly and preventing it from spreading. The stakes were high and we learned quickly to put the wet stuff on the fire. We worked in harmony with the FDNY and usually got to the fire before them because our trucks could operate in the sand. It would be rare to have a house fully engulfed but if we did, we would work concurrently to put the fire out and wet down other homes downwind to stop the advancement. We understood early that working together was the only way to go. Both organizations were extremely professional and we worked well together. One could think of FDNY as a major league team whereas a volunteer fire organization within the city could be viewed as minor league. Many members of the nine volunteer companies within New York City were hoping to be one day drafted into the big leagues.

In the early days the department was active during the summer months. At the end of summer, the three local volunteer fire departments would erect wooden structures made from driftwood to resemble a home. They would set it ablaze and each department would race to extinguish the fire. The purpose was to give the residents confidence that they were in safe hands. In the late '50s the department became an all-year organization to accommodate the families that began to move there year-round. My family was one of the first one hundred families to do this. We all knew the importance of the firehouse to the community and we knew it was an honor to serve. My family and many other local families provided the manpower which formed the backbone to the department.

Back in the days before cell phones and pagers, we were called to duty by an intricate siren system similar to an air raid siren from a World War II movie. One blast of the siren represented a medical problem and summoned the ambulance corps. Two blasts indicated that we had an auto accident. Three alarms meant a structural fire. On rare occasions one could hear six consecutive alarms and this meant an evacuation was in process. When the fire siren would sound, members would drop what they were doing and run to the firehouse to get their equipment and jump on one of the rigs. The calls could come at all times of the day, and no one ever got used to the midnight calls in the middle of winter.

Our track record was good with few injuries or losses from major fires. On the average throughout the year, most of our calls were minor incidents like arcing wires, odors of gas and grass fires. It was very rare to have a major structural fire; however, each newly elected chief would do a risk assessment of potential hazards in the neighborhood and develop scenarios and training to prepare the department for any eventuality. We had a great reputation in the community and the people were thankful and generous with their donations. Our funding came mostly from donations and fund raisers like the summer dance and the sale of chance books. Occasionally, we received grants from public agencies.

My year as a probie seemed to last forever. I became an expert at cleaning bathrooms and taking out the garbage! The probie is the low man on the totem pole and usually gets the unpopular assignments. We learned quickly that teamwork was the best way to get a job done.

The phrase "many hands make light work" was frequently spoken. I was later promoted to firefighter and the time flew by. Before I knew it, it was June 1971 and I was twenty years old and graduating from college. The war in Vietnam was in full swing and staring me full in the face. I always wanted to become a pilot, so the day after graduation I signed up with the United States Air Force to join the Air Rescue Team and become a rescue helicopter pilot. I submitted a request to the Point Breeze Fire Department for a leave of absence due to military service and it was granted. Though I was gone, the firehouse and the members would always be in the forefront of my thoughts. I became a frequent visitor when on leave from the military and presented my future wife, Nancy, with an engagement ring on the engine deck of our firehouse in 1971. Anytime I visited Breezy, I would always manage to re-acquaint myself with the department. In 2004, I moved back into the neighborhood and re-activated my membership with the PBFD. This time, due to my age, the training drills were more difficult.

CHAPTER 4

Becoming the PBFD Fire Chief

FRANK FARRELL, A good friend of mine, was a past chief of the department. One day he said to me, "the best job in the firehouse is to be the past chief. In order to become the past chief, you have to be the chief."

Upon my return to the PBFD, I was quickly elected to lieutenant and then moved up to captain. In 2010, I was elected as chief. It was a great honor and I promised to do my best. I was no longer a young man and stepped into the job at the ripe old age of sixty. Another former chief and good friend warned me that leading a volunteer organization would be the biggest challenge of my life. As I look back on all of the events during my tenure, I would say his advice was all too accurate.

Unlike some paid full-time fire organizations where chiefs are selected from a competitive written test and then sent to a specialized school training in that position; in most volunteer fire organizations the members

elect their officers. It is not a popularity contest but an honest assessment of whether the individual would be successful in the position. It certainly helped that I did my probationary year and later served as a lieutenant and captain within the PBFD.

All prospective fire chiefs spend several years as entry level firefighters. The process for me to become a fire chief started when I was a probationary and basic firefighter, in my teenage years. Education is an important element. I held a master's degree with an extensive background in management. My life experience helped me to be prepared both physically and mentally for the job. As chief, I knew it was important to surround myself with good people. A chief must be relentless in creating innovative ways for making the community safer. I knew I was fortunate to have a large talent pool from which to select. To become a chief, it requires a deep sense of obligation to serve the community and the fire service. I instinctively knew how to be a successful chief; I needed the trust of others. In order to earn and keep their trust I needed to always communicate honestly and demonstrate a reliable decision-making capability. I knew that reliable decision making could lead to saving people's lives. I felt confident that I had the character and thick skin to handle some of the negative aspects of the job. Based upon my past leadership roles, I viewed myself as a subservient leader who worked for the people. I didn't view myself as the type of leader who made the people work for me. My leadership abilities would be the most important tool in my role as fire chief.

Like all chiefs before me, we wanted to have a quiet watch. Unfortunately for me that wasn't in the cards. The first thing I did in my new position was to make a risk assessment and to determine our vulnerable areas. Most of my background was in aviation and I was currently working as a senior management official in the Federal Aviation Administration and worked many accident investigations. Unfortunately, one of those accidents would happen close to home. On November 12, 2001, an American Airlines Flight crashed in the Rockaways in close proximity to Breezy Point. After take-off from JFK International Airport, the tail section of the Airbus aircraft separated from the fuselage and parts of the aircraft rained down on the neigh-boring residential community of Belle Harbor. The PBFD was one of the first trucks to arrive on scene. As an aviator I knew that if the aircraft stayed airborne for one minute longer, it would have hit Breezy Point with devastating results. JFK International Airport was ten miles away and jetliners were constantly taking off or landing, with many of the aircraft flying over our neighborhood. The close proximity of the wooden homes in Breezy Point mixed with heavily fueled aircraft constantly overhead was a dangerous combination. If a plane pancaked into Breezy Point like it did in Belle Harbor, we would have dozens of houses on fire all at once. After confer-ring with the officers on my staff, we decided that we needed to train for a multi-house fire of approximately thirty homes. This was significant because all of our past training was to prevent the multi-house fire from happening, but under the assumption it would start with one home. Now we were admitting that there was a possibility that events out of our control, like an airliner crash, could cause an apocalyptic fire and wipe out the neighborhood. This would be a major undertaking and too difficult for a small local volunteer fire department.

I used my connections at the FAA to prepare for such an event. We realized that many small-town fire departments surrounding JFK were in the same position, so I approached my immediate boss, with an idea to create "A First Responders Course for Air Disasters." He gave me the green light to next approach our good friend Regional Administrator Carmine Gallo who liked the idea and helped to devel-op a partnership with the Port Authority of New York and New Jersey (PANYNJ). They already had the responsibility for Airport Crash Fire and Rescue, and most importantly they had the experience. A course was developed and early on a Sunday morning it was presented to a group of volunteer firefighters from the departments surrounding JFK. Ironically, we were preparing for a multi-house fire from a plane crash and shortly thereafter we were destined to experience an enor-mous residential fire.

The year 2010 was the Centennial Year of the Department. Our first challenge was to locate and invite all of our past members to the Centennial Dance celebrating our legacy. We booked the nearby Silver Gull Beach Club and planned a major celebration. I borrowed an idea from the military and developed a challenge coin for the Point Breeze Fire Department. The idea was met with some resistance since it was mostly a military tradition, but I thought it was a great way to create our own brand and we coined a term that would be prophetic, "Breezy's Bravest." Initially I had around a hundred created and it was an excellent way to create goodwill and to give people a token of our appreciation at the party. We honored our past chiefs and our members with fifty or more years of service. We also invited our community leaders to join us in the celebration. Fun was had by all.

In 2011, we received a new replacement truck. It was a modern, state-of-the-art apparatus with many computers, bells and whistles. We purchased it with the generous donations from the community and with an allocation of funds from the New York State Senate. The chassis was made by International Harvester and the truck was designed and built by a Pennsylvania based manufacturer named KME. It was specially equipped with four-wheel drive to accommodate the special needs of our community, specifically driving in the sand and narrow alleys. Our senior firefighters had solicited ideas from the rank and file and shared these ideas with KME. The truck it replaced was to be retired which was named after one of our previous chiefs and was called "BIG JACK" after Jack Crowley who was so loved that we decided to continue with his name on the new truck. He had passed, but his widow and two sons were still with us.

It is a tradition in all fire departments that when a new truck is delivered, the department will have a "wet down" prior to entry into service. So again, we gathered our friends and public officials and our chaplain, Father Brian Jordan, OSF, gave a blessing. I made what is to be remembered as a speech that was too long. Father Brian, a Franciscan, was dressed in his brown robes and was almost fully baked in the hot June sun by the time I finished saying my words. He reminds me of this episode nearly every time we meet. As penance I can say that I have never duplicated this effort and nearly all of my speeches are now concise. My only defense was that I loved both the department and its members, it was easy for me to go on and on and brag about them.

Later in that year we were deeply saddened by the passing of one of our members, Jim Hampton. He was one of our officers and died suddenly in a non-job-related death. It was especially tough on our younger members as they didn't have much exposure to death. I met with Father Brian and we managed to hold a memorial service on the engine deck of the firehouse. The service had a dual role to accomplish. It was the department's way to treat our member with dignity and respect and it was also a way to show the younger members how we honor the lives of those who dedicated their lives to serving others. Father Jordan's eulogy was spot on and once again he overachieved.

My term in office as chief of the department included a steady stream of major events. I was not destined for any quiet time during my watch. In the summer of 2011, we were faced with the threat of Hurricane Irene. The area had not been hit with a hurricane for a long time. The media tracked the storm and as it approached the northeast nearly everyone was in a high state of alert. The press hyped the storm and from all reports it was to make a direct hit upon New York City. Mayor Bloomberg ordered an evacuation of all coastal areas and the Emergency Management System was activated. The unending flow of over-hyped news reports really had the people amped up. Common wisdom dictated that since we hadn't had a real hurricane in several years, we were overdue.

I called for a meeting of our members to discuss a plan of action. Our first item of discussion was whether we should follow the

Mayor's evacuation order or ignore the order and stay to protect the community. It was agreed that since we held a charter to operate as a volunteer fire department, we had a legitimate reason to ignore the evacuation order. We then developed a plan to determine availability of firefighters and staffing needs during the approach and aftermath of the storm. We located cots and sleeping bags and purchased food to last several days. We inspected and prepped our firefighting equipment to ensure our readiness. The trucks' fuel levels were topped off and all batteries were charged. When the necessary precautions were accomplished, we set up a meeting with the other two volunteer fire departments in the community as well as the leadership of our community's management team. We compared notes and reviewed plans so that we would work as one team and maximize our effectiveness. Hurricane Irene was predicted to make landfall in the middle of the night. Our members were ready and on full alert when at the last moment Irene took a turn and gave us only a glancing blow. We experienced coastal flooding, high winds and some heavy rain. The members of the PBFD stood bravely in the face of the storm and were relieved when it changed course. The biggest event that happened that night was an electrical transformer explosion. We responded to the call and cordoned off the area until the utility company arrived and resolved the problem. Many of us had hunkered down and sheltered in place awaiting Hurricane Irene and expecting apocalyptic results. The false alarm created by Hurricane Irene would set up a scenario that caused more people to ignore the warnings of future storms.

One of the key responsibilities of any chief is recruitment. With the advent of computer games and mobile devices it was very difficult to recruit able-bodied young members. I was fortunate that the prior chief was able to attract a strong group of young people. They ranged from high school and college students to young men working blue collar jobs waiting to be called for civil service jobs such as a firefighter within the FDNY or a police officer within the NYPD. They were a good bunch of young men and even though they liked their games, they also liked the idea of saving other people's lives.

Training young firefighters to run into a burning building as everyone is running away is not an easy task. To do this without any monetary rewards sounds like an impossible task; however, about 75% of fire companies in the United States are volunteer organizations. Our drills continued to be rigorous as led by our officers and members who were retired from the FDNY. We also took the extra step to enroll our probies in the Nassau County Fire Academy for specific courses. It was a big commitment for a young person to make the decision to become a volunteer firefighter and not everyone completed their probationary period. The tradition of the probie being the low man on the totem pole, as I experienced so many years earlier still continued. They were expected to constantly keep the place clean and do all of the unpopular jobs. I also recruited a member a few years older than myself to work with the fire police and manage traffic during fire calls. He became one of my best success stories. He had a variety of careers that helped to make him a positive role model to our younger members.

As a former chief warned me, managing a volunteer workforce was to be the greatest challenge that I would experience. He was right and despite having held key leadership positions in the military and federal civil service, I had my work cut out for me. The group recruited shortly before my watch worked diligently during their probie year. They were a cohesive group and retained their friendships when they were outside of the firehouse. I came to nickname them as the *core group*. They were the heart of the organization and I knew that many of them would grow to become future leaders. We purchased a flat screen TV set that accommodated both cable TV and computer games. We also set up a dart board. I wanted to create an environment that would draw the members to the firehouse and make them feel valued. The firehouse would be a place to go to in their off hours and also a place where they could respond quickly to emergency calls.

My first problem arose when we didn't have any probies in the training pipeline. I noticed that several of the senior members who were used to having the probies cleaning up the area were now sitting on the sidelines waiting for the new members to continue to do the unpopular work of cleaning up. It started to become a morale issue among the core group and I knew if it was allowed to fester, it would negatively affect retention. I privately spoke with past chiefs and members of both groups asking for advice. I quickly realized that this was a generational issue.

I needed to find a way to make equitable distribution of the work. I came up with a plan and called the members together to share the plan. I first assured them that the probies of the future will continue with the tradition of doing the unpopular work. In the meantime, each of us will be asked to do ten small tasks to keep the place clean when we arrive at the firehouse. If they chose to do a large work item like taking out a big garbage bag that would count as five or six items. I explained that it would be on the honor system and that everyone had to participate. This included the officers and me as chief. I made a point to allow them to see me take out the garbage and do some other unpleasant tasks. Before I knew it, morale had improved and the place was looking sharp.

I developed a series of animal metaphors that helped to gently get my message across. I can't remember all of them but they can. They now call them Martyism's. We had an early morning work party and as a group they looked worn out. It was apparent they were out late the night before. I joined the group and said, "It's difficult to soar with the eagles when you spend the night hooting with the owls."

Several days later I came into the back room and the discussion suddenly shifted, for my benefit, to the subject of grilling birds such as owls and eagles. I quietly smiled to myself and avoided the rest of the conversation. I knew both groups, the seniors and the core group, were outstanding people and, if necessary, I could lead them into hell and back. Little did I know that was to be our destiny.

In August of 2012, my initial two-year term was up. I was easily re-elected to a one-year term. Our department's by-laws called for an initial two-year term and then you could run for a consecutive one-year term. Ironically, in just two months I would learn being "easily re-elected" would be a call to use all of my talents in order to overcome my most difficult challenges. After the initial three years, if someone wanted to do a challenge run, you were not able to run. It was a great way to ensure turnover in the leadership ranks and to bring in fresh new ideas. I had at least a year left to continue to raise the bar of excellence. If there was a challenge to me to run for a third term it would be up to the new guy to continue the efforts. The place was looking really good. The plan to take on ten little tasks upon arrival was working really well. I decided to expand the "Rule of Ten" to all of the equipment and appliances within the firehouse. If something was not operational, it would go on the List of Ten. We would focus on either fixing the item or replacing it. If a cabinet door was broken, I would call upon Firefighter Marty Walsh, who was a carpenter, to get a work party together to fix it. If one of the toilets was clogged, I would call upon Firefighter Rick Savage, who is a plumber, to get a work detail together and fix the problem. The List of Ten was very active and, before long, everything seemed to be functioning properly. The place was in ship shape and running like a top.

Past Chief Ed Wolfe ran a beverage machine for a small profit and was able to create a "Back Room Fund" to help support the member's morale and welfare. I saw that we were throwing out some empty cans and losing the five cent deposit so we started saving the cans and collecting the deposits. We set up work details to cash in the cans and then turned the money over to the Back-Room Fund. Eddie Wolfe knew that some of our members were down on their luck and he was quietly able to loan them some money from the fund. It was readily apparent that the morale was improved. The friendly critical banter was ever-present and if the members weren't picking on someone, they didn't like him. The needs of the people, equipment and the building were being addressed and we were ready to handle any challenge thrown our way. It looked like my second watch was going to be quite different from the first and I was looking forward to enjoying the quietude. Once again, I would be denied the opportunity.

August 2012 was a special time for me; I retired from my 41-year career as a federal employee. I would now have a considerable amount of time to pursue my interests which were my family and the firehouse. I booked several vacations for November and December. Around the middle of October, I received a phone call from my brother John who was a sixty-year-plus member of the department and a former PBFD Fire Commissioner. He met an old friend at the gym who said that the Guinness Beer Company had a promotion going on that they were giving away samples of their new beer to first responders and members of the military. The Giveaway had some restrictions to follow. It couldn't be given to minors, couldn't be sold and the recipient had to accept the entire load of beer from an eighteen-wheel transport. It would consist of seventy-two pallets and an unknown number of cases. It was a challenge we were ready to take on. We didn't have the room to store all the beer and developed a plan to notify our fellow volunteer fire departments and some veteran and military organizations of the Great Guinness Giveaway. We were lucky and came up with a fork lift and operator. At the pre-arranged time as the eighteen-wheeler's cargo of beer was off-loaded, we had a half mile long line of assorted fire trucks, ambulances and military style vehicles that were patiently awaiting their distribution of Ireland's famous product. By nightfall we were exhausted from loading the vehicles and we were ready for some relaxation.

Later that night I made sure we had a list of firefighters to be on call and the rest of us set out to sample the Guinness family's new product of lager beer. One of our new probies, Chris Warren, was a city music teacher. He set up his equipment and started to play some classical Irish music. The beers were iced and the beverage began to flow freely. The men were relaxed and proud that we were able to conduct the "The Great Guinness Giveaway." They knew that the beer went to good people who devoted themselves to saving other people's lives. I looked around the back room with quiet pride toward the members of our team. The opportunity to relax was a blessing but I left after a few. I knew that the next morning would bring another opportunity to soar with the eagles. Several months later, after feeling the full effect of Hurricane Sandy, my daughter Erin said, "The next time the good Lord delivers an eighteen-wheeler full of beer you guys better brace for what comes next."

Very quietly, over the horizon several thousand miles away, the hot air from the Caribbean Sea was mixing with the warm ocean waters of the Atlantic Ocean to form a dangerous low-pressure system. After this system collided with another low-pressure system it would eventually become known as "Hurricane Sandy, The Superstorm." The weather professionals of the National Oceanographic and Atmosphere Administration (NOAA) projected a path that would miss New York. The weather officials of the European Climate Prediction Center forecasted that the storm would make a direct hit on New York City. Unfortunately, the Europeans were correct.

As with Hurricane Irene, the media weather outlets were reporting gloom and doom stories that had everyone scared. Because Hurricane Irene fizzled, many of us felt that Hurricane Sandy would do the same. Despite the feeling that this storm was being over-hyped and driving people into a frenzy, we reviewed our plans and duplicated the efforts by which we'd prepared for Hurricane Irene. We set up for a twenty-four-hour operation and went shopping for food, cots and other essentials. Our firefighting equipment was inspected, fuel tanks were filled, and batteries were charged. The dividends on our continuous improvement plan and our plan to fix or replace everything on the list of ten was paying off.

It was Sunday night and the storm was not expected to arrive until Monday evening. Our preparations were accomplished in a short time. We then went to the community's boat storage area to commandeer a lightweight, shallow draft boat. We didn't find one; but I was relieved, because we never trained on boats. On our return trip to the firehouse, we drove near the shoreline and could see the surf was angry and already encroaching on the beaches. The sea gulls were all leaving the peninsula and heading to the mainland, just as the fisherman warned so many years ago. We knew we were in for a bad time. We were passing one of our favorite neighborhood watering holes, the Sugar Bowl, and I decided to stop in for a quick visit. I met with the owner and made small talk. This building was a treasure chest filled with memories. I was there when Neil Armstrong and Buzz Aldrin landed on the moon in July 1969. I knew the exact place where I was standing when the lunar module touched down and it would be a pleasant memory whenever I stopped by. I didn't know it at the time but this would be the last time I visited the "Bowl." It would be destroyed in less than twenty-four hours.

There was an eerie silence in the neighborhood. Not many people were out and about. The emergency siren system was constantly going off, signaling the order for evacuation--blaring six long sirens calling for everyone to leave. It reminded me of the movie "Planet of the Apes," when the air raid sirens would alert the people to go back to their cave-like dwellings. The parking lots still contained many cars and this was a big concern. If one was to evacuate a neighborhood, why would you leave behind a car? I was pretty certain that many people chose to ignore the order to evacuate and sheltered in place, and there were still about a thousand cars throughout the property. We knew then that the false alarm presented by Hurricane Irene had a major impact on the decision-making for this new threat.

Twenty-four hours before Hurricane Sandy made landfall the European and American weather services were in agreement. New York City would receive a direct hit. The Triboro Bridge and Tunnel Authority announced that it would close the Marine Parkway Bridge between Brooklyn and Queens at 6:00 pm on Monday, October 29th. This, combined with the FDNY decision to move all equipment and personnel off of the peninsula, was devastating. Their decision was based on protecting their assets. We suddenly felt isolated and alone.

Our plan was to shelter in place and to be available if a fire started or if needed to rescue any of our residents. No one wanted to admit it, but the faces of some of our team betrayed their apprehension. I knew if I looked at a mirror of my own reflection, I would have to add my name to the list. For a critical period of time the three communities of Roxbury, Rockaway Point and Breezy Point would only be protected by the three volunteer departments from these communities. Earlier we were suffering from being macho and in denial. In a few hours we were due for a rude awakening.

We had several guests visit us in advance of the storm. Some were parents checking on their sons. The local New York State Assemblyman and good friend Phil Goldfeder dropped in two hours prior to the storm's arrival. He came from a family that volunteered for an EMS ambulance organization and knew of the culture of life-saving volunteer organizations. His visit raised our morale and he toured our now 24-hour operational facility. He wished us luck and started on his journey home ten miles to the east. I was concerned for his safety. Fortunately, he made it home without incident.

By sundown our preparations were all done and we started to prepare dinner for the crew. Mike Schramm was not only the editor of our local newspaper, but he was also a graduate of the Johnson and Wales Culinary program. At key moments like this he would jump in and cook a special meal. The morale of the team was always at the highest when he presented us with his culinary delights. This turkey dinner would be cooked but go uneaten. The arrival of the storm and the serving of the meal happened at the same time. Timing is everything.

CHAPTER 5

Into The Blue Yonder

AIR RESCUE CREED

*It is my duty as an Air Rescueman to save life
and to aid the injured.
I will be prepared at all times to perform
my assigned duties quickly
and efficiently, placing these duties
before personal desires and comforts.
These things we (I) do, that others may live.*

MY LIFETIME OF experiences within the Air Force, mostly with floods, fires and storms prepared me for the disaster of Hurricane Sandy. I spent over thirty-one years, either full or part time, in the USAF, Air National Guard, and the USAF Reserve. Twenty-five years were spent as a rescue helicopter pilot and six years as an emergency disaster management officer. As a young man I had a major interest in aviation and knew I wanted to fly. In 1971 when I was about to graduate from college, I volunteered to become an Air Force Rescue Helicopter Pilot.

I signed my contract with the Air Force the day after graduation. The day before I left, we had a big farewell party at the clubhouse celebrated by friends and family. Before the party was over my friends presented me with a Revell plastic model kit of an Air Force RB-66 jet. The RB designation stood for reconnaissance/bomber and it resembled a fighter aircraft. The container was small and easily fit into my suitcase. I brought it with me on my new journey and I read all the details of the aircraft and learned some obscure info that included the fact that the aircraft could carry up to four crewmembers. The information I learned about the RB-66 would have a big impact later when I flew my first air rescue mission.

This training pipeline was more than two years long. My initial training focused upon leadership, management and discipline. We were first taught to command people and knew later we would command air machines. Some of our core values were: "Service before self" and "Excellence in all we do." Special emphasis was placed on strong personal integrity, constant situational awareness and critical thinking skills. We were also trained on "Followship" and respecting the chain of command.

In flight school we started out on small aircraft and progressed to much larger machines. Our flight instructors placed major emphasis on training for inflight emergencies. We learned to always have a plan and be able to adapt to new situations. It was mandatory that we stay calm no matter how devastating the malfunction and to think clearly no matter how much adrenaline our body was producing. Our job was to restore order out of chaos and maintain control. It was important that we protect the lives of the people on board and also protect the aircraft so that it would fly and fight another day. Decision-making and critical thinking skills were among the requirements of a pilot. Later in my career, I would be making decisions while in command of a combat helicopter, flying fifty feet above the surface at 150 knots. In that environment all those decisions needed to be correct.

The Air Force Air Rescue Service is a world-wide operation and our unit insignia depicts an angel encircling the planet Earth with its wings. Our motto was, "These Things We Do So That Others May

Live." It was a great mission and an easy motto to live by. After earning my wings, in September 1972 I was assigned to fly local base rescue at the USAF Flight Test Center at Edwards Air Force Base, California.

Edwards was an exciting place. The test pilots were engaged in the development of jet powered high-speed aircraft. They were busy flight-testing the fourth generation of fighter aircraft like the legendary F-15, F-16 and A-10 fighters, and they were also developing the B-1 Bomber and the X-24B.

My experience as a young firefighter helped in this assignment. My rescue crew on the UH-1N helicopter was pilot, co-pilot, hoist operator, medical technician and aircrew firefighters. We were one of the few places in the USAF where firefighters were a primary member of an air rescue crew.

Providing hover cover for firefighters in burn pit.

We normally carried two firefighters and they wore the silver bunker suits that protected them from extremely high temperatures. In the event that the pilot failed to eject and was trapped within the "fire ball" of the aircraft, we externally carried a one thousand-pound "Fire Suppression Kit" (FSK) to the accident site. The FSK was released near the aircraft wreckage and the firefighters used the hoses and tank filled with 83 gallons of water and foam. They then created a path to the cockpit to rescue the pilot. Part of the procedure was to have the helicopter hover-taxi over the firefighters into the fire to assist them to reach the cockpit. As pilots we had to learn how to fly into the fire in both day and night operations. Night Ops was particularly challenging with the flames licking the night sky. It was difficult to maintain a stable hover. We needed to monitor the temperatures with special concern for our fuel tanks. It was a very dangerous mission that was

eventually discontinued. A risk assessment found it to be too dangerous and it could not be justified.

Besides losing the firefighters as crewmembers, our med techs
were being replaced by pararescue men returning from Vietnam.
They were combat veterans who never liked rear echelon people calling the shots. Although they followed established guidelines there
were times when they had the common sense to go ahead without
asking for permission and instead would ask for forgiveness. They
were nicknamed "PJ," and were part of the USAF Special Operations
Force. It was a highly qualified career field and they were the elite of
the Air Force. Many of them were highly decorated from their combat
experience in Vietnam and one of them received the Medal of Honor

My first rescue as a newly minted co-pilot was for an RB-66 which
was traveling through our area. It departed from a nearby overhaul facility and experienced an inflight emergency, crashing seventeen miles
off base, near the town of Rosamond, California. We landed near the
wreckage and located the pilot and co-pilot who'd successfully ejected.
We were about to lift off and get them to a hospital when I remembered
that the aircraft could carry more than two crewmembers. Both pilots
were incapacitated and unable to tell us there were still crew members
on board or in the area. I told the aircraft commander not to leave yet.
"There may be an additional crewmember in the area." It turned out that
there was one additional crewmember that we rescued. My aircraft commander was surprised and asked me, "How did you know?" Normally
new pilots are to remain quiet with very little input because of their in-
experience. I explained that at my farewell party, in Breezy Point, before
joining the USAF, I was given a Revell plastic model kit of the RB-66
and the info was included in the attached aircraft sheet. That innocent
gift helped to provide me with information that saved a third crewmember's life. A long time ago I gave up on thinking some things were just
coincidences.

In 1974, the USAF was evaluating the BD-5, built by the Bede Corporation, to be used as a USAF pilot training aircraft. It was a single seat jet experimental aircraft with a confined cockpit. It would be later known as the world's smallest jet. The commandant of the Air Force's Test Pilot School was flying the aircraft when he experienced a catastrophic inflight emergency and in attempting to land, he rolled it up and crash-landed on the runway. As the alarm sounded, we did a scramble start and arrived on-scene within minutes of the crash. Our PJs were extricating him from the tiny aircraft and discovered that he was not wearing the regulation leather flight boots required to be worn by all Air Force airmen. The pilot was unconscious and it was obvious he was wearing sneakers. The lead PJ came back and informed me of the situation and noticing that I had same size feet he asked to borrow my flying boots as a loan to the commandant so he could avoid any unnecessary questions. They hid his sneakers and tossed my boots onto his stretcher. I flew my first bare foot rescue and delivered him to the base hospital. Later we found out he had a special waiver to fly in sneakers and not leather boots. We initially had a hard time explaining but everything worked out fine. In 1979, the author Tom Wolfe would write a book called "The Right Stuff." It was an accurate portrayal of life at Edwards and the pioneering spirit of these pilots.

On New Year's Day in 1975, I received a call while on standby alert at home. A two-year-old boy from Boron, California, managed to get into the parent's medicine cabinet. He mistook their medications as candy and was in critical condition. The isolated location of Boron lacked the equipment or expertise to handle this emergency. We were called to Medevac him to the Children's Hospital in downtown Los Angeles. We scrambled and arrived at Boron in record time and when we were preparing to depart for LA, I experienced my first case of the rear echelon folks trying to micromanage the mission. The watch officer at the rescue coordination center ordered that the father of the baby could not accompany the child on the aircraft. We did our best to get the father on board the helicopter but the headquarters people were adamant. We landed the baby on the rooftop helipad of the Children's Hospital in less than an hour, but it took the father nearly three hours to make the trip by car. Without a signed parental consent form, the doctors had to await the father's arrival before they could begin treatment. Fortunately, the child survived and we were credited with a Save. It was the first rescue of the New Year and it received a lot of visibility within the global rescue community. I walked away from this experience knowing that operations manuals were meant to be guidelines and that common sense should prevail. I knew in the future, in a similar situation, I would ask for forgiveness rather than permission. This new philosophy came in handy on my next mission and would follow me throughout my life.

In 1975, I left active duty and joined the Air National Guard. My new unit was the 106th Air Rescue Wing in Westhampton Beach, New York. The unit was changing missions from air defense interceptor mission to an air rescue mission. It was an honor to be part of a team to create a new rescue wing. I quickly checked out as an aircraft commander on the HH-3E. It was one of the largest helicopters and was equipped with a mid-air refueling system for long range missions or for flights in "bad guy" territory where gas stations were not available. Our unit also flew the HC-130 transport aircraft which acted as our air refueling tanker.

Whether a first responder is a civilian or works in the military, many would agree that some of the best planned operations can quickly go awry. Sometimes the easiest mission can go to hell in a handbasket in a short amount of time. It takes a lot of work and creativity to bring the situation back under control and turn the effort into a success. Very few first responders have been involved in a rescue effort where they get it under control only to discover that overnight the situation has turned into a true disaster.

In mid-November 1981, the Cold War between the United States and the Soviet Union was heating up. President Reagan had just called the Soviets "the Evil Empire." Historians would later refer to this period as the Second Cold War. Newspaper headlines carried stories that reflected the increased tensions. "Aeroflot Penalized for Errant Flights." "U.S. Government Suspends Flights into United States Airspace by Soviet Airline Aeroflot for a Week." Apparently, Aeroflot Airlines, departing from JFK International Airport, deviated from their flight path and overflew the US Submarine Base at Groton, Connecticut. They were reported using the civilian airliner to take photos of the new Ohio Class of submarines. In turn, the Soviet Union banned all Pan Am flights into the Soviet Union.

On the evening of November 16, 1981, I was called at home and asked to fly a MEDEVAC (Medical Evacuation) of a critically ill patient from Stony Brook Hospital on Long Island to New York University Hospital on the east side of Manhattan. Any mission that we got involved with was of a life-or-death nature. If we succeeded in recovering the survivor alive or safely delivering the patient alive the organization was credited with a "Save." The rescues at sea were frequently dangerous and dramatic. The hospital medevacs, on the other hand, were less dramatic and even though the helipads weren't the best planned aerodromes, they weren't as dangerous as hovering over a bobbing fishing boat. The squadron helicopter crews began to refer to the saves earned on hospital medevacs as "cheap saves."

Upon arrival at the base, I found the entire crew present and the aircraft thoroughly pre-flighted and all necessary paperwork prepared. The East 34th Street Helipad was advised of our arrival time and the weather was excellent for our nighttime flight. "What's the medical situation of the patient?" I asked. The supervisor of flying responded, "The patient has an aortic aneurysm. He's 76 years old and they are afraid the aorta will rupture at any time. They have doctors and an operating room standing by at Bellevue Hospital. One doctor, a nurse and a respiratory therapist will accompany the patient. They want us to make the transport because we'll be the fastest; and if the patient has any complications while in route the PJ and medical people will have enough room in the back of your aircraft to work on him." Within an hour from the time of initial notification the aircraft departed Suffolk County Airport on the first leg of its mission. The first destination was the tiny helipad adjacent to the emergency room of the University Hospital.

The landing there was uneventful. Once the aircraft was readied, the medical team raced the patient to the awaiting rescue vehicle. "Crew, this is the pilot. As soon as the patient is on board, we'll secure the aft ramp and start the rotor engagement checklist. Once everyone is strapped in, we'll take off. Prior to landing here, I noticed the weather to the west looked a lot worse than forecasted. Let's get out our maps and charts in order to prepare for marginal weather conditions." The crew fully understood. We had all lost friends when a squadron helicopter and its crew perished in marginal weather conditions in 1978.

"New York Approach Control, this is Air Force Rescue 783," I announced over the radio as we became airborne.

"Roger Air Force Rescue 783. New York approach," they responded. "Air Force Rescue is lifting off from Stony Brook Hospital inbound to the East 34th Street Helipad."

I was advised that shortly I would be turned over to LaGuardia Approach Control. Besides being a native of Long Island, I had been flying in the area for six years. As I called out the towns we were passing over, my co-pilot, John Schoeck, would cross reference the checkpoints to his aeronautical chart and navigational instruments.

"Nissequogue, Northport, Huntington," I announced, sounding much like a train conductor on the Long Island Railroad. Visual navigation on a dark night is accomplished by identifying lights from towns and villages and by land and water formations. As we approached Huntington, we became aware of the fact that the cloud layer was descending, forcing us to cruise at a lower level. "LaGuardia Approach, this is Air Force Rescue 783. We're leaving one-thousand feet for seven hundred feet."

"Roger," came the reply from the controller who was busy talking to the air traffic arriving and departing from LaGuardia. I called for the descent checklist and simply informed the crew that we were descending to maintain visual flight conditions.

Schoeck and I reviewed the procedures for inadvertent entry into instrument meteorological conditions (IMC). Helicopter flight in marginal weather at night can deteriorate in an insidious manner. As the visibility is reduced, more time is spent by the aircrew in interpreting the limited information; and the crew may not be fully aware of an even greater reduction of forward visibility. When the cloud ceiling is lowered, the aircraft is forced closer to the ground and ultimately closer to the obstructions. Schoeck and I conferred and decided that if we encountered bad weather we would turn around and return to safer conditions. In the event the weather deteriorated behind us, we would either land the aircraft or get an instrument clearance to fly in the weather.

As the aircraft flew over the western portion of Bayville, I was forced to continue descent to 500 feet. The Long Island shoreline was free of obstacles. Prior to reaching Oyster Bay one of the nurses announced on the intercom that she "was running out of gas." She was

Photo of the HH-3E used on The Rescue Over the Red Mansion.

referring to the patient's oxygen supply. His medical condition required a constant supply of oxygen. "I need some oxygen; I need more gas!" said the nurse in a high-pitched tense voice. Pararescueman Kevin Kelly came on the intercom. "PJ to Pilot. The patient is running out of oxygen. I have a small bottle but that should last only ten minutes."

I responded, "Roger PJ, we're about twenty-six miles out; see what you can do to make it last. The weather looks pretty bad up ahead. We might have a delay."

As we approached the mouth of the Hempstead Harbor, Schoeck announced that the altitude was about 300 feet and the airspeed was 60 knots. The mouth of the harbor was slightly over one nautical mile wide but we were unable to see the other side. We realized we were in a freak weather pattern, most likely in an unforecasted fog. The weather fourteen miles west had unrestricted visibility. We chose to fly south into the harbor with the hopes of seeing the western side of the harbor and resuming our westward course. As we entered the harbor, I passed over a mansion that was brightly lit. I briefed the crew that if the weather deteriorated any further, we were going to return to this area and use the brightly lit mansion as a reference point as we coordinated an instrument clearance. The weather did fail to improve and we returned to the mansion that acted as a beacon in the night. We flew two additional circuits over the structure and picked up an instrument clearance to fly directly to East 34th Street Helipad. I performed a maximum climb departure. The lighted mansion gradually disappeared as the helicopter with its roaring engines began its ascent into the blackened mist. The air traffic controllers gave us priority treatment and we were able to land at the heliport before our limited supply of oxygen was exhausted. It was 1:00 am when I finally returned home. I found my wife Nancy, at the front doorway. "Hi, how come you're still up?" I asked.

"The weather around here was awful about nine o'clock; you couldn't even see to the street."

"The weather wasn't too bad," I lied. "It's a shame that they mix such an imprecise science as meteorology with such an exacting science as aviation," I philosophized. "Why don't we get some rest and I'll tell you about the rescue tomorrow." I always postponed giving her the details. On various occasions, if she had known the truth, she might not have let me do the things I liked best, and that was flying aircraft and saving people.

While at the kitchen table the next morning, I received a call from my immediate supervisor, Colonel Giere. It was unusual for Giere to call me at home. "Marty, tell me about your rescue mission last night," he began. I was becoming alarmed. It was just too unusual. Something was certainly afoot. No one had ever called to congratulate either me or anyone else in the squadron regarding the success of our missions.

"It wasn't much," I said. "We picked up the patient and medical team at Stony Brook and dropped them off at East 34th Street Helipad for Bellevue Hospital. The weather got bad enroute and we had to pick up an instrument clearance, otherwise everything was fairly routine. It was a cheap save."

Then very calmly Col. Giere said, "Tell me what you know about the Russian Ambassador." Initially, the question seemed absurd. What would the Russian Ambassador have to do with last night's rescue? I paused, and after thinking about the question, I responded. "Frankly, I don't know anything about the Russian Ambassador. We did initiate our approach to the East 34th Street Helipad abeam the United Nations Building. It is quite possible that he may have seen us go by his window."

Col. Giere asked, "Marty, when you picked up your clearance, would that by any chance have been around Glen Cove?"

"Yes, as a matter of fact, it was."

"Marty, have you listened to the radio yet this morning?" Giere asked. I quickly replied that I hadn't.

"They are carrying a story about a helicopter that buzzed the residence of the Russian Ambassador to the United Nations in Glen Cove last night. The news reports are saying that the helicopter was so low that it put a hole in the Ambassador's roof. A lot of people are very upset. Evidently the Russians are filing a complaint with the United Nations. The Director of the FBI, not an FBI agent, but the director himself called and wants to know what you were doing in the area last night."

I replied, "If we put a hole in their roof, we should've put a hole in our aircraft. You should have someone inspect the aircraft." "We're in the process of doing that right now," said Giere. "In light of these circumstances, there are a lot of questions to be answered. I want you to report to the base as soon as possible. We'll schedule someone else to take your flight this afternoon." I told him I would, fearful that I would never be allowed to fly again. 'Colonel Giere, I would be less than honest if I didn't tell you I am both shocked and quite scared."

He replied, "Marty, in light of these circumstances, you have every right to feel the way you do." Giere added, "We both do."

As I hung up the phone, my wife could see my ashen face. "What's going on?" she asked. "Apparently, a helicopter buzzed the Russian Ambassador's residence last night and it is a good chance that it was my aircraft." "Oh my God," she said echoing my sentiments and reflecting my shock. Again, I hastily changed into my Air Force uniform. "I've been asked to come out to the base to answer some questions. It should prove to be very exciting. Evidently, the director of the FBI has called."

Realizing that pinching myself would not remove me from this nightmare, I turned on the car's radio. Regrettably, the radio was tuned to a local news station. Immediately the announcer's words told me there was no need to listen any further. When one inadvertently is responsible for a news event, the only value of hearing it through the media is to determine the accuracy of the reporting. Sadly enough, the news was reporting that a lost helicopter buzzed the Russian Ambassador's residence at Glen Cove, and how international tensions were increasing.

Upon my arrival at the base, I was ushered into an office where the rest of my crew was already assembled in front of Col. Giere and his assistant. An uncomfortable silence permeated the room. Giere rightfully assumed the role of a military commander. I instinctively knew that Giere would play a tough adversary role and I hoped he would be fair.

As I entered the room Colonel Giere said, "Come in, Captain Ingram, have a seat."

There were two things wrong with this statement. Over a year ago, I was promoted to the rank of major. The other problem with his greeting was that there were no other chairs available in the room. The only area to sit down was a well-worn carpeted area in front of the operation's officer desk. I would always remember this experience as the epitome of the term "being called in on the carpet."

Giere prefaced his remark by informing my crew of a series of events that helped to aggravate the situation. Only two days prior to our rescue, Russia's Aeroflot Airlines was restricted from operating in U.S. airspace due to overflights of American defense facilities. The Russians reciprocated by restricting Pan Am from flying to Moscow. On the night before Air Force Rescue 783 flew over the compound, someone had fired a weapon toward the residence. Later, the Russians charged American terrorist activity. The FBI initiated a full-fledged investigation of the incident. After Colonel Giere made this announcement, he addressed my crew. "Your sense of timing is truly incredible. It is widely rumored that the Russians equipped the civil aircraft belonging to Aeroflot with cameras. It may not be a coincidence that Aeroflot strayed over Groton, Connecticut at the same time the U.S. Navy is about to launch a new Ohio Class of nuclear submarines. You should consider yourselves extremely fortunate you weren't shot down."

I silently agreed.

The questions began. There was no pulling of punches. Giere lived up to the Squadron's management philosophy of tough but fair. "Why were you so low?"

"I encountered weather that was not forecasted," I responded.

"Did you check the weather?"

"Yes sir, here is a copy of the weather briefing sheet."

Giere continued with the cross examination. "How low were you flying?"

"Over water, at the lowest we were three hundred feet: over land, the lowest we were was four hundred feet." As the questions progressed it became more apparent that they were following the British rules of justice, that being the assumption of guilt until proof of innocence.

"Were you lost?"

"No Sir, I knew exactly where we were. I simply did not know who I was over and what events transpired before I got there." "Do you have any ties with anti-Russian organizations?"

I was growing uncomfortable with both my seat on the carpeted floor and the line of questioning. I stood up and addressed my crew's makeshift tribunal. "Gentlemen, through all this confusion, I think we have overlooked some very important details. My crew was not out on an evening's joy ride. Each and every one of these people responded from their homes during their off-duty time in order to help someone who was in need. We did not operate that low by choice but by necessity.

"Regrettably, the place we chose to orbit was a target of some recent violence that has led to increased international tensions. Perhaps these preceding events and the resulting increased security could explain the reason why we chose this particular area. By illuminating their compound, the Russians inadvertently attracted an aircraft that was in need of a prominent visual reference point. I also failed to mention that while we were in the orbit over the Russian compound, I actually had our gear down and if we didn't receive the instrument clearance, I planned to land and deliver the patient to a medical facility by a ground vehicle. It is quite possible that we may have landed on the Ambassador's property. Considering the difficulties, we encountered and the success that my crew achieved, I feel that they should be presented with a more favorable reception. Furthermore, I would like someone to inform the Russians of how valuable they were in this particular rescue operation and relay our sincere thanks."

Giere was able to visualize and understand what happened. It was now his job to properly pass this information along so that when it reached the Russian Ambassador, he too would understand. Hopefully, after a proper explanation the Russians would withdraw their United Nations complaint and maybe the international tensions would ease.

Before releasing my crew, Giere informed us that an inspection of our aircraft revealed nothing out of the ordinary. Before dismissing the crew, Giere suggested that we call home and warn our families that there might be an influx of press inquiries and to refer all contacts to our public affairs office. The next morning, I approached Colonel Giere and asked how it was going. "We passed your explanation up the chain of command and the Russians acted favorably. Once they heard it was a mission of mercy, they immediately dropped any complaints. They were fair and understanding in regard to the whole episode. In a couple of days this whole affair will most likely be forgotten. I can assure you that this episode won't negatively affect your career or that of your crew. It is best to let the dust settle and perhaps someday in the future you can tell the real story. The irony is that in the heat of the Cold War your crew and the Russians inadvertently worked together to save a person's life."

Due to the nature of our business, all of the rescue crewmembers were close. One of my most difficult rescue missions was the rescue attempt of one of our own. We were all devastated when on October 30, 1991, one of our helicopters ditched sixty miles out to sea in a storm during a long-range rescue attempt. The storm was initially known as "The No-Name Storm," though later it was called the "Halloween No Name Storm," and then after Sebastian Junger wrote his book, it was called "The Perfect Storm."

I was at home and received the call at 9:00 pm, within one hour of the crash. My orders were to launch at 3:00 am. I was the designated aircraft commander and our job was to rescue our five downed aircrew members. I tried to get some sleep but only managed to say a lot of prayers. I was making deals with God and promised to be a better person if we could recover our crew. Right at the liftoff, our Ops Center received a call that the US Coast Guard vessel Tamaroa, was on-scene making the rescue. My mission was aborted and the crew of the Tamaroa recovered four of the five-man crew. They did it at night, against tremendous odds in the middle of the storm. Pararescueman Technical Sergeant Rick Smith was lost and despite two weeks of intensive searches he was never recovered. It was devastating and any future illusion of our own invincibility was shattered. This was a hard lesson to learn and certainly humbling.

A year later, in December 1992, I reported to the base for a routine training flight. When I arrived our "green phone" hotline to the United States Coast Guard Rescue Coordination Center was calling for a long-range oceanic rescue. The sailing vessel "Lightfoot" was two hundred miles south of Long Island inside another "no name storm." This one would later be called the "Great Nor'easter of December 1992." In reality it was another "no name hurricane."

We quickly put together a rescue package of the MH-60G helicopter and HC-130H airplane as an aerial tanker. Our new helicopter was fully equipped with modern area navigation and we also had our night vision goggles (NVGs) since the tail end of the mission would be under night conditions. As luck would have it our area navigation system was not working, but we decided to rely upon the C-130 to navigate to the last known coordinates. We flew through intense weather bands after which we experienced a drop in atmospheric pressure. It was like Dante's "Inferno" and each weather band represented another circle of hell. The weather was so intense that when the C-130 was turning in a left bank, the strong winds caused the aircraft to almost become inverted at low altitude. The conditions were exceeding our aircraft's capability and we were forced to abort the mission. A hoist pickup would have been impossible and the survivors would be safer on board the sailboat. The two sailors had locked themselves in their cabin, written their names on their arms and lashed themselves to their vessel. They were eventually rescued by a cargo ship. The storm had a big impact upon me personally., I had a greater respect for Mother Nature and I became closer to God. They say "in war there are no atheists in a foxhole." I would testify that the same goes for those who are inside air pockets within a hurricane.

In August of 1995, the Central Pine Barrens of Long Island experienced a major brush fire that extended from Rocky Point to Westhampton and covered twelve square miles of wooded area. It actually jumped over the major four-lane roadway called Sunrise Highway. The fire would be later nicknamed "the Sunrise Wildfire." Over two thousand volunteer firefighters from 174 volunteer fire departments across Long Island fought the battle. Governor Pataki and Senator D'Amato were involved in a political quagmire trying to get aerial water tankers and smoke jumpers to fight the fire. Normally this equipment was reserved for fighting wildfires in our National Forests, so the fire raged for several days without any federal support.

Several helicopters equipped with water buckets were doing their best to extinguish the fire but the fire seemed to have a mind of its own and spread without the help of the wind. It also broke out behind them and destroyed nearly a dozen fire trucks. Our MH-60G was equipped with advanced technology but we were not equipped with water buckets to fight a fire. Initially we were disappointed that we couldn't contribute. Ironically, we had some specialized equipment on board our aircraft that would help to save the day. One of our new high-tech enhancements was the Forward-Looking Infrared (FLIR) Camera pod. We were trained on how to use it and the common application was to develop a video output on a cockpit screen to be used in night or limited visibility operations. Any other application was up to our imagination. This equipment was like a large-scale version of the Thermal Imaging Camera (TIC) popularly used by firefighters around the world and could see the varying levels of heat.

I was flying with Captain Graham Buschor, who was a survivor of the Perfect Storm ditching. He was rescued by the United States Coast Guard vessel Tamaroa. We were surveying the fire zone when I brought our aircraft to a stationary hover 100 feet above the ground. I asked Graham to adjust the camera pod directly beneath us. Immediately, to our surprise, we could see a sub-surface web of hot spots connected by lines of fire that were not visible to the naked eye. Apparently, the root system of the Pine Barrens carried flammable pine sap which helped the fire to continue to spread underground. We contacted the other helicopters with the aerial water delivery kits and shared our discovery. We set up a procedure in which we directed them where to drop their water. The water bucket drops extinguished the underground fire even in areas where it looked like there was no fire at all. We finally knocked down the fire, although two days later the aerial water tankers arrived and staged a demonstration water drop. The news media was on hand and filmed the show. They mistakenly gave them credit for extinguishing the fire.

In 1996, I was assigned to the First Expeditionary Air Rescue Wing at Incirlik Air Base, Turkey. At that time Saddam Hussein was using poison gas on the Kurdish people of northern Iraq. Each day during Operation 'Provide Comfort', a coalition of Turkish, British, French, German and American fighter aircraft would patrol the area to ensure the Kurdish people were safe. My job was to rescue any of the crew from coalition aircraft in the event they were shot down and help the Kurds as necessary if they were attacked by their own government. It was a combat assignment with low intensity.

Upon my return stateside, I transferred to the USAF Reserves and continued my service in a non-flying capacity. I became a member of the Air Force National Security Emergency Preparedness Office (AFNSEP). We created training exercises that tested existing plans for a variety of disasters. I was assigned to the First Army Headquarters and acted as the Air Force Liaison Officer to the Federal Emergency Management Agency (FEMA). The First Army handled all disasters east of the Mississippi River and was headquartered at Fort McPherson, Georgia. I had to learn the entire disaster response network and the way they do business, besides learning Army vernacular and their culture and traditions. The response to Hurricane Andrew (1992) was a fiasco and the whole response system was overhauled. They created a dozen Emergency Support Functions (ESFs) and grouped functional areas to provide federal assistance to the individual states. During a disaster I would be assigned to the First Army, FEMA or the State Operations Center and my job was to obtain USAF resources to support the different ESFs. In this new job, I would again be involved with disasters that would involve floods, fires and storms. In my new capacity, I was given a high-level authorization letter allowing unrestricted travel in the event of a national emergency. This letter would prove invaluable during the attacks on September 11, 2001.

My first disaster response was the North Florida Wildfire. High temperatures and no rain created drought conditions and turned the entirety of Flagler County into a tinderbox. The county and state response quickly collapsed and the federal system came in to help. I was able to get fire trucks from California flown to Florida in C-5 Transports. Because of the sandy topography of the northern Florida surface area, I had to locate D9 Bulldozers that could operate in the soft environment. I identified some Air Force resources in Alaska that were being used on the tundra and had them flown to North Florida. It was interesting to be part of such a large-scale team. Normally a disaster is handled at the county level. When it becomes too much for the locals, the state comes in. Lastly when the states can't handle the situation, the federal government becomes involved. This is all thanks to the Stafford

Act of 1988, which allows the Federal government to come in and systematically bring assistance to restore order. It all starts when the President signs a "letter of declaration of a major disaster." My understanding of the National Disaster Response system would later help in our recovery after Sandy.

On September 5, 1999, Hurricane Dennis hit coastal North Carolina twice and left the area saturated with overflowing rivers and streams. Soon after, on September 17, 1999, Hurricane Floyd made landfall near Cape Fear, North Carolina. It was a category four hurricane but upon landfall it was downgraded to a category two storm. Hurricanes bring either major wind or floods. Very rarely would a hurricane carry both. Floyd was carrying both coastal flooding and torrential rains. The combination of the flooding from both Dennis and Floyd caused the Neuse and Tar Rivers to rise 41 feet above flood stage. Many people east of I-95 were now victims of what is considered a seven-hundred-year flood. Thirteen years later, in my capacity of the PBFD Fire Chief, I would face what would be considered another seven-hundred-year storm as Superstorm Sandy blasted its way across the Rockaway Peninsula.

I was working the command post at First Army while my good friend, Lt Col Tom Henderson (USAF) was working the North Carolina Emergency Operations Center (EOC) in Raleigh, North Carolina. We got along really well. He was a former fighter pilot and he knew I was a former rescue helicopter pilot. He reported that at the state level it was pure pandemonium. With the swollen rivers from Hurricane Dennis and the new rain from Hurricane Floyd they estimated that nearly 2,000 people were now trapped in their attics and were about to drown from the rising waters.

He said, "You were in the rescue business. How can we save these people?"

I gave him the location of Army and Air Force Rescue assets along with state and local resources. I outlined separate radio frequencies, ingress and egress routes and specified altitude separation. I told him we had a C-130 at Patrick AFB, Florida that could air-refuel the Air Force helicopters and also act as the Airborne Mission Commander to keep everyone separated and avoid any mid-air collisions. I also wanted the night-vision goggle-equipped aircraft to operate at night. He quickly hung up and I was bombarded with many other issues. We were both multi-tasking.

Normally, the state EOC submits a written request that is signed off by the Defense Coordinating Officer (DCO). Then a Request for Assistance (RFA) would be forwarded to the First Army and approved by the commander and FEMA would assign a cost accounting code. After the RFA is approved, the "green light" is given and the RFA is assigned as a "tasking." I never saw Tom's RFA come across my desk. Several critical hours passed and finally Tom was able to get back to me by phone. Proudly, he explained that the C-130 from Patrick AFB was about to land at a North Carolina Air Force base and he had other helicopters already engaged.

I said to Tom, "I didn't see your RFA to the First Army and FEMA." He came back with, "Was I supposed to do that? It was your plan and I figured it was the only approval I needed."

My stomach was doing flip flops and I began to feel ill. I explained to him the process and told him to get the RFA signed by the DCO and get the request up here, ASAP. I always knew the line between a court martial and a medal was a very thin line. Neither one of us wanted any medals, but a court martial would be a certainty if one of those aircraft crashed. A short while later despite jammed phone lines, he told me that we had a big problem. He presented the request to the DCO, who is an Army officer. Surprisingly, the DCO disapproved of the plan, not knowing it was already executed. Again, I got that sick feeling. As I was talking with Tom, the DCO called me directly. He started off with, "Ingram, I have this plan" and goes on to outline in detail the plan that Tom and I hatched. I acted as if I knew nothing about it.

When he finished, I said, "Sir, if you get this RFA up here quickly we might be able to save the two thousand people who are trapped in their attics." The mission was a success and Tom and

I dodged a big bullet. We were never court martialed but we were awarded a few medals.

Not since the British Army besieged Washington DC and destroyed the White House in the War of 1812, has our capitol been under attack. On September 11, 2001, terrorist hijackers commandeered four commercial airline flights and proceeded to crash two of them into New York City's Twin Towers and one into Washington's Pentagon. The fourth was unable to hit its intended Washington target because the hijackers were overrun by angry passengers and they crashed in a field near Shanksville, Pennsylvania.

Shortly after American Airlines Flight 77 crashed into the Pentagon, I was called to active duty by the Air Force National Security Emergency Preparedness Office and ordered to report to the Pentagon. I was living near Charlotte, North Carolina at the time and the best way to travel was by car. I had my National Security authorization letter next to me and made the trip in record time. The roads were virtually empty. Most people were at home, focused on the news or on their telephones, worried about the safety of their loved ones.

After a brief stop at Langley AFB in Virginia, I reported to the Pentagon early on the morning of September 12th. As I entered the Pentagon, the destruction from the crash of American Flight 77 was evident. The smells of jet fuel and burnt rubble permeated everything. Never in my wildest dream did I ever think the Headquarters for the Department of Defense would be attacked nor did I ever think I would be reporting to work in a building that was just attacked in our nation's capital. Response plans called for the relocation of personnel and equipment to work outside of the Capital District after an attack. Fortunately, these plans were not followed. The "optics" would have sent a wrong signal to our fellow countrymen and, by working in the same building, which was targeted by our enemies, this showed our awakening resolve and let them know we meant business.

At the Pentagon there was a single point of entry and everyone entering needed to sign in a log sheet and present proper identification. I had to wait for an escort and I had a terrific opportunity to witness the human traffic reporting for duty. Many of them were service members who were involved in a variety of military functions that would ultimately determine our appropriate military response. It was amazing to see people going to work while others were carrying out body bags and parts of the American Airlines Boeing 757 airliner. In addition, there were emergency responders, morticians and construction people reporting for duty to stabilize the conditions within the building and specifically around the crash site.

My job as an Emergency Preparedness Liaison Officer (EPLO) was to not only coordinate inbound Air Force resources to each of the crash sites but to also prevent unauthorized Air Force resources from participating in the recovery. Everyone wanted to be involved. At the same time, too many people and their associated equipment could saturate the disaster area and bring with it a deadly gridlock. I was assigned to a command post someplace in the basement of the Pentagon. Normally, when a commercial airliner crashes, the entire area is cordoned off to restrict access. In this scenario we knew we were somewhere underneath the crash site going about our important business. Because of the attack, many of the utilities like Heating, Ventilation and Air Conditioning (HVAC), sanitary plumbing, electrical and communications were greatly challenged. The command post was staffed 24 hours a day and it eventually operated for several months. I worked for the first week and did twelve-hour shifts. Most of our support focused on New York City. Initially, we had fighter aircraft overflying New York's skyline to film the area for the creation of high-level briefings for senior military officials. We received word that the fighter aircraft were causing people to panic. Many people were fearful of a follow-up attack. We quickly identified some light general aviation aircraft equipped with cameras belonging to the Civil Air Patrol to do the job. Because of their slower speeds they were able to get higher quality photos and they didn't scare anyone.

On my first day at the command post, I learned that the people at "Ground Zero" in New York City wanted a tent city. I knew this request had to be in error. When I was stationed in Turkey during "Operation Provide Comfort" we had a tent city and it was huge. New York City didn't have enough open real estate to accept such a large entity. Everyone in the system was trying to please the people in New York and the Air Force was about to ship the package without completely vetting the request. I knew this order needed to be validated. I called the New York City Command Post and spoke with the person who made the request. I explained the normal size of the average tent city and he was astonished. He definitely didn't want this type of package. It rained the day before and all they wanted was a small "party tent" at Ground Zero, where workers could take a break and stay dry. Now we knew exactly what they wanted and after a few phone calls we identified a local vendor who had exactly what we needed. Next to me, there was a Navy Disaster Officer who was diligently working to get a Navy Hospital ship to sail to New York Harbor. The next day the national news had a video of the Navy's USNS Comfort, a hospital ship sailing into the harbor and the little party tent at Ground Zero to keep the workers dry on their breaks. My Navy counterpart and myself gave cheers and high fived each other in jubilation of our accomplishments.

In anticipation of many casualties from the attacks on the World Trade Center an entire USAF Medical Wing in Texas, self-initiated a mobilization to a nearby Air Force Base in New Jersey, expecting an onslaught of medical emergencies. The sad reality was that most victims were mortally wounded and would not need medical care. The other problem was that a request had not been made and validated. Although the action was well intended it had the potential to overwhelm the system. The unit was placed on stand-by at their base and they were denied entry into the Area of Operations (AO).

During and after Superstorm Sandy, I was involved with several important civic organizations in the Rockaway Peninsula. I realized that we were fortunate to have many of the key people in leadership roles who were highly qualified and had a lifetime of skill sets that would help the eleven communities to survive the storm and restore the neighborhoods to better conditions than existed before Sandy's visit. People like New York State Assemblyman Phil Goldfeder, and many others within civic organizations and cooperative boards used their leadership positions to work together and achieve many great things. I often wondered at how fortunate we were to have them in these positions in advance of the disaster. Was it a coincidence or something else?

My experiences within the military prepared me for the challenges that Superstorm Sandy would present. This, combined with the core group's formal training at the Nassau County Fire Service Academy, our firematic training drills and their personal drive, prepared us for our ultimate challenge: the historic flood, and fire within Superstorm Sandy.

CHAPTER **6**

Anticipation

A Prayer for Meteorologists

Dear Lord,
Watch over me as I practice my craft.
Give me peace as I go through my day.
Grant me wisdom to make good choices
so that my understanding of the weather
reflects the truth of the day.
Let me always remember the privilege I
have to use my free will and creativity
as I help to forecast the weather in the
world you have made.
Amen
-Jay Greginski

MANY OF US are in denial about the next weather disaster to come our way. We've surmised that since we experienced our most recent hurricane, we aren't due till some distant date in the future. After Hurricane Sandy, we heard that it was a "seven-hundred-year storm." So, for many of us, we falsely believe that it can't happen again in our lifetime.

The hurricane season in the Atlantic Basin area goes from June 1st through November 30th. The United Nations World Meteorological

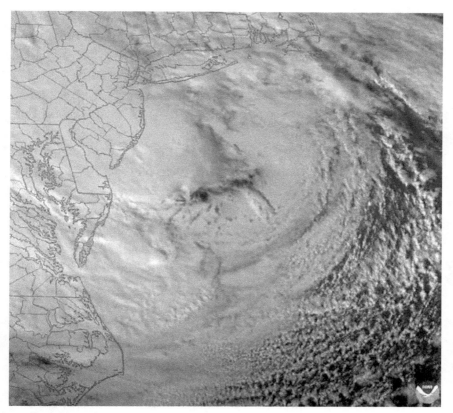

Satellite photo of Hurricane Sandy

Organization with their member nations develop a list of names for each season for each basin where tropical cyclones are generated. Lists are created six years out and each list carries at least 21 names. These lists are repeated every six years, with new names only being added when a storm's name is retired due to being deadly or extremely damaging.

Our expectations begin to rise as the news media starts to report the development of the tropical storms. Through satellite technology and charts that depict the possible tracks and strength of the developing storms a clear picture is presented to a viewer. The media continues with their focus on the storm's activities on a daily basis adding greatly to everyone's anticipation. Typically, after the storms first make landfall, videos of the devastated areas are shared by the media and now many people who are in the potential path of the tropical cyclone start to elevate their concerns. Their anticipation now turns into fear. Supermarkets throughout the affected area are packed with shoppers who clean off the shelves of essential items. Much of the food purchased in haste will be thrown away as power failures sweep the area and the food spoils. People become glued to their radios and televisions to hear the latest word on how the storm is developing and where it is possibly going. The news media also adds nicknames to the already-named-storm to further hype the situation. Names like "Frankenstorm," "Perfect Storm," and "Superstorm" are added to distinguish this storm from past monsters that invaded our calm world. The best way to anticipate these disastrous weather events is to develop individual plans, community plans and educate ourselves regarding the types of help to expect from the local, state and federal governments.

On an individual basis, we should all have a plan to evacuate to a safer place further inland, on higher terrain. It's best to coordinate with a family member, a friend or a hotel for a place to stay on a short-term basis. The plan should include the decision to make an early evacuation and have considerations for senior citizens, the sick and even our pets. Emergency planning checklists can be obtained on the internet. Valuable tips such as sharing your status with relatives can be helpful in reducing the stress of the event. Many people purchase NOAA hand held emergency network radios and are able to hear important weather alerts and announcements.

On a community level, advance planning can help to designate shelters and resource distribution centers. Conduct local training drills and exercises, to include after-action-reviews to seek ways to improve. They should also educate the local people on the importance of obeying an evacuation order. If they insist on staying, suggest they leave markings on their body, so as to help in identifying their body in the event of a death.

Communities should move in the direction of resiliency. Raise electrical panels and elevate homes in the flood prone areas. As stronger storms become more frequent, they will be traveling further north. Greater winds will create greater damage to roof structures. The adaption of reinforced roof beams, clips and straps to increase the uplift resistance is important. Ensure that critical first responder apparatus and equipment are located in an elevated area and can avoid flooding. Personnel and equipment should be able to shelter in place, in their own resilient fire stations. The idea of relocating of personnel and equipment to higher ground can be dangerous because conditions may not permit a timely return to protect lives and property. Communities should consider developing vertical garages for a dual purpose to serve not only as a routine parking location but to serve as a protective zone during a hurricane.

Hurricane plans should not only consider the event itself but also address key issues in the aftermath and recovery. Breezy Point was becoming grid locked while storm debris was being stacked up in critically needed sand lanes and other main thoroughfares. The New York City Department of Sanitation (DSNY) was the unsung hero of the recovery effort after Superstorm Sandy. They transformed a large unused parking area at nearby Riis Park and turned the area into a staging area that acted as a transfer-recycling station. They worked around the clock to remove the debris and separated material so that it could be re-purposed. Apparently, they had pre-existing contracts with salvage companies and recyclers who carried away most of the material to be disposed of properly. Concrete debris material was placed in specific piles and then ground down to be made into clean gravel. There were many cars destroyed by the fire and flood and these vehicles were quickly removed for proper disposal. Hazardous building materials were identified, separated and stored in a safe manner and were disposed of properly.

After action studies conducted by local, state and federal authorities, major and minor projects should be identified to improve resiliency and help to mitigate damages in future events. Long term plans should include self-help projects. Following Superstorm Sandy, Breezy Point built their own system of sand dunes that has already helped to protect the community in several coastal flooding events since Superstorm Sandy. For bigger projects, like building coastal flood protection like jetties and piers, the Army Corps of Engineers can be an outstanding agency for local communities to work with in building resiliency.

Scientists and engineers have explored various means to limit the strength of Tropical Cyclones. They have looked at seeding the clouds, towing icebergs, pumping cold water from ocean depths to the surface, adding an oil slick to the top surface water to deny buildup of energy in the water. They even considered using nuclear weapons to disable a hurricane. Engineers are exploring ways to pump a mix of gases into the upper atmosphere that will act as a sun shade to cool down our oceans and deny the hurricanes their much-needed energy. Many of these efforts are complicated and may have unintended consequences.

After some necessary coordination with officials of the National Oceanic and Atmosphere Administration (NOAA), I was able to interview Senior Hurricane Specialist Robbie Berg of the National Hurricane Center (NHC). I shared my background both as a pilot and

Our good friend, meteorologist Champion, received a Peabody Award for his coverage of Superstorm Sandy.

as a fire chief with him and identified myself as a "weather geek." Ever since I became an Air Force helicopter pilot I was fascinated by weather. We hit it off well and he admitted that meteorology was his passion and he too was a "weather geek."

I started the interview by asking him, "So how was the name Superstorm Sandy developed? Was it developed by the NHC or did it come from outside your organization?" He responded, "In the weather world, all hurricanes are called 'Tropical Cyclones,' and for each hurricane we develop a thorough Tropical Cyclone Report (TCR). This storm acted very differently from past hurricanes. As it was almost abeam New York, it took a sudden left turn and now it took aim at central New Jersey and the New York Harbor." We both agreed that the media most likely dubbed the term "Superstorm," since Sandy had lost some of its hurricane characteristics.

I knew my next question would be sensitive but I felt it needed to be asked. In my best gentle manner, I asked him, "I know that the main U.S. weather tracking models had Sandy staying east of New Jersey and New York City. On the other hand, the European Centre for Medium Range Weather Forecasts (ECMWF) model predicted the storm would make a left and turn directly for the east coast exactly as it happened. What happened?"

His response was well thought out and impressed me as being honest. He explained, "Weather models aren't perfect. There are many factors that go into the algorithms that we use to make our predictions and if we miss some key information or plug in skewed data the computers can produce inaccurate projections." Silently, I knew from my flying experience that on a much smaller scale, we received some inaccurate data. I learned at an early age that the science of meteorology was still developing and could be referred to as an imprecise science.

Robbie further explained, "All weather models have their day in the sun. For Sandy, the European model was the most accurate. For other storms the U.S. models can be the most accurate. It's up to forecasters to assess and weigh the various model simulations and make a forecast that involves their best judgment of what will happen. Although we usually agree on forecasts, the Europeans had it right on this night. "There have been other examples when we disagreed that the NWC was proven correct. Making consistent accurate predictions on hurricane movements is a very difficult process. As technology and computers improve, we all get better."

He further added, "As the storm approached landfall Sandy lost some of its tropical characteristics. Although the winds stayed at hurricane levels and the barometric pressure remained low, the storm maintained its strength and was still dangerous. A coastal low pressure in the upper atmosphere merged with Sandy to help give it, 'superstorm status.' The tropical nature of the storm turned to non-tropical. The inner core of the storm is normally warm but as Sandy made landfall the core turned cold. It was a matter of semantics. Technically, Sandy was no longer a hurricane but it still carried destructive forces stronger than most hurricanes. When Sandy moved inland, there was already cold air in place over West Virginia. The storm tracked over West Virginia and dissipated over Michigan. Everyone in the area experienced an early season snowstorm."

I asked him if he thought that we were now seeing an increase of hurricanes due to climate change or a change in cyclical weather patterns. Robbie said, "The number of storms has not increased, as far as we can tell. What is changing is the rapid buildup and strengthening of storms. The hurricanes are producing greater tidal storm surges. They are moving slower and delivering a greater amount of rainfall, creating coastal and inland flooding."

He went on to explain that the two greatest hazards of a hurricane are wind and water. Water is the most dangerous. Hurricane Sandy started in the Caribbean Basin and ended in northern Michigan. It killed 147 people, 72 died in the United States and of that number 41 people died from water-caused crisis. Sandy was over 900 miles wide and at landfall it caused a nine-foot storm surge."

I found information regarding the New York Bight that described an even more dangerous picture. The area called the New York Bight is the triangular indentation along the Atlantic coast of the United States and extends northeasterly from Cape May Inlet in New Jersey to Montauk Point on the eastern tip of Long Island. It's the place where the east coast changes ninety degrees from north/south to east/west. The change in direction of the coastline causes the bight to act as a Catcher's Mitt. To make matters worse Sandy chose to arrive at full moon high-tide.

Robbie went on to explain, "Since we know the dangers associated with tidal surges and coastal flooding, we are collaboratively working with state and federal emergency managers in developing unique Storm Surge Risk Maps. These maps will identify coastal zones at risk. We are always improving our modeling and tracking procedures. We are now using Microwave Satellite Data to get a better look inside the storm. After Sandy we made some significant changes. We developed 'storm surge watches and warnings' to explicitly warn people of possible hazards. It's another tool in our toolbox."

Our conversation addressed some of the efforts to minimize the strength of hurricanes. We both agreed that the risk was too great and the unintended consequences could be many. Robbie said, "Hurricanes play an important role in replenishing drought-stricken areas and in balancing the heat of the upper atmosphere. With the advent of satellite technology our best tool is early notification. We have a lot of early warnings. We need to learn to live with the storms." As our interview came to a close, I thanked him for his help. I left with a strong feeling of appreciation for the men and women of the NHC and applauded their professionalism and dedication. Without their expertise we would never be able to anticipate the deadly disasters that routinely visit us.

At the time of Sandy, it was considered to be the second most expensive storm in hurricane history. It is now back to number four. Greater storms and inflation will bring new storms that will push Sandy further back in the line. The National Hurricane Center in conjunction with the World Meteorological Organization (WMO) continues to develop six rotating alphabetic lists of twenty-one names. The list now alternates between male and female names. The names of significant tropical storms are retired. The name "Sandy" will never be used again. When one looks at the risks from floods, fires and a superstorm, many of my friends are astounded that the community of Breezy Point did not lose one person during that awful event.

The best way to minimize the dangers of hurricanes is to learn to co-exist with them. Proper building codes that address the hazards of high winds and flood waters is a starting point. Education of the public is important to gain a greater awareness that these storms may be more frequent and stronger. The best thing we can do is to anticipate the threat.

CHAPTER 7

The Fire

AT THE TIME, no one knew how the fire started, though later we would learn that it started as a result of arcing after the salt water came into contact with the electrical lines. Arcing is caused by electrical voltage discharge coming into contact with salt water. We also learned that the Long Island Power Authority (LIPA) shut down the power grid on Fire Island but failed to do so on the Rockaway Peninsula. This eventually became the basis of a major lawsuit. At present, however,

the firestorm was raging. The sky was filled with softball-sized embers that were constantly streaming across the night sky from the fire zone. It looked like a meteor storm and if it was a National Geographic video in the comfort of my living room it would have been enjoyable to watch. I ordered all of the firefighters to make sure their visors were down and that their helmets were securely buckled. The fireballs were exploding all around us as they hit the water. I knew it wouldn't take much to set a house on fire. We were all on Unit 8, the SAND FLEA. The truck was over twenty years old but we were running it like a race horse. We were evacuating the survivors and driving through deep water, filled with debris. We had the last survivors in the back seat and our firefighters were on the step on both sides of the truck holding on to whatever they could grasp. I knew we were breaking nearly every safety rule in the book but the situation was grim and it required assuming extra risk. The firestorm was intense. I continued to have the sick feeling that this whole area would be charred rubble in a short time. Mike Schramm's house was directly to the west of the firehouse. We started to leave the area and I remembered Mike said he was keeping his two dogs in the house. I shouted out to him, "Mike, where are your dogs?"

He said, "They're in the house."

I stopped the truck and said, "Mike, get the dogs and bring them with us."

He asked, "Why?"

"Don't worry. I'll tell you later." I didn't have the heart to tell him I really believed the whole place was going to be leveled in a short time. We put his dogs in the back with the other survivors and continued on our journey. The Sand Flea now looked like Noah's Ark as it plowed through the flooded area with its precious cargo of survivors, firefighters and animals.

As we started to leave, we received a call to go to the northwest side of the property to rescue a senior citizen suffering from Alzheimer's disease. His house was flooded and he needed medical attention. The sidewalk was impassable and a wheel chair would be out of the question. He lived at the end of the flooded block and would need to be carried.

Tim Dufficy was in the driver's seat and he already made several trips to the public shelter at Saint Thomas More Church and I was now sitting in the front officer's seat next to him. All of his previous trips were upwind of the firestorm and smoke plume. Now he had to drive downwind and penetrate the firestorm. The smoke was both blinding and suffocating. Our eyes were watering and black snot was coming out of our noses. We all had trouble breathing and visibility out the front windshield was zero. It was impossible to look out the front window. The headlight and high beams were completely ineffective and the red emergency lights were reflecting off the nearby smoke clouds merging with the ever-present red fireballs. It was useless to try to look out the front of the rig. He started to drive with his head out the side window.

No matter how hard we trained, nothing would prepare us for this night. We needed to become creative and find new ways to get the job done in the face of formidable odds. Tim is a veteran firefighter and applied his creative problem-solving skills with ease. When he couldn't see out the front window, he stuck his head out the side window and drove the truck by looking down on the side of the truck. When the smoke got too heavy and he couldn't see the road from the side, he ordered the night "fighter lights" in the back of the truck to be positioned face down. Normally these lights were used during a job to illuminate the fire area but now we seemed to be engulfed in fire and he was using these lights to help us navigate out of the fire and smoke.

There would be many other examples of opportunities to use his critical thinking skills to solve problems during the night. He drove the truck at a very slow speed, fully aware that there would be hazards and obstacles in the roadway. I did my best to peer out the front window and spot the obstacles. Several times I called out "stop" and the firefighters positioned on the side step would run out and clear the way. I was amazed at the force of the storm. Somehow a one-hundred-pound concrete flower pot was repositioned to the middle of the road and we were lucky to stop in the nick of time. Traveling through the black smoke plume was like living a bad dream. Everything seemed surreal. Within seconds, because of the limited visibility, strange objects would suddenly appear. If we didn't respond properly and quickly, we ran the risk of putting the truck out of commission.

Tim did a great job of driving the truck forward by looking backward. As we emerged from the black cloud, we saw what was to be our worst fear. We were only one block from the survivor's location when we discovered the fire had jumped. It was on the northwest side of the property about a mile away from the fire zone. The house was near the intersection of Bayway Walk and Bath Walk. It was also two houses from Tim Dufficy's home. The front of the house was totally engulfed. Apparently, a fireball lodged into an area on the house after it was super-heated by the smoke plume. It didn't take much to get it engulfed. Our challenges were becoming very extreme. We now needed to prioritize which challenge would come first. We had several survivors and some dogs crammed into the back of the truck who needed transport to a safe area. We had a senior citizen with dementia who needed to be evacuated. We also had a monster fire a mile to the southeast, threatening the entire community. And now we had a house fully engaged in fire on the north side of the property.

On a normal night a single house fire would be a real threat. Initially, Tim was concerned that if we fought this fire and not the major fire, someone may be critical that we prioritized this because we were trying to save his house alone. I debunked his concerns and stated that the rest of the homes had to be super-heated and were ready to go. If we didn't put this fire out, the house would act like a starter kit for yet another major embroilment. We had a direct radio line to FDNY Dispatch and Tim reported the new fire. At that point we didn't know when FDNY would be able to get back on the peninsula. Sebastian Danese, a volunteer firefighter and an off-duty NYPD officer, was riding on the step over my shoulder and listened to the discussion. I knew we had to extinguish this fire first and I didn't care if someone at a later date would be critical. It was the right thing to do. My new plan was to extinguish this fire, collect the survivor we came to rescue and then deliver all of them to the secondary public shelter. After all of that, we would position ourselves in front of one of the biggest residential fires in New York City history. Our challenges were overwhelming.

Dufficy pulled up to a nearby hydrant. I had Firefighter Danese along with another off-duty NYPD Officer, Firefighter Pat Dooley, grab the nozzle from the hose bed. Mike Schramm, Kevin Hernandez and I would stretch the hose from the hydrant to the fire. Mike was a giant of a man with endless energy and strength. After Mike stretched the hose, I ordered him to extricate the victim. If this fire got out of control, our medically disabled senior citizen survivor was immediately downwind of this house fire and he would be doomed. I later heard reports that when Mike carried our survivor down the sand lane in a fireman's carry, he looked impressive, like Saint Christopher carrying the child across the river.

Out of nowhere two retired FDNY firefighters appeared. Knowing that we had a full night of work ahead of us, I immediately deputized them and gave them their assignments. In our teenage years, I was friends with these men and knew they were highly capable firefighters. Our new additions, Rich Jackson and Raymond Hendry jumped on the nozzle. Dooley went into the structure and did a house search and also evaluated the extent of the fire inside the house. We were lucky, the fire was just on the outside of the southern facing structure. The problem we had now was low water pressure. This problem would haunt us all night.

Both Hendry and Jackson didn't waste any time letting me know their needs. They were both seasoned firefighters and knew that at the right time, the f-bomb was the right word to use to convey the seriousness of the situation. I ran to Dufficy, who was now working as the Motor Pump Operator (MPO) to provide assistance. He already received the message and developed a plan to connect to a second hydrant. The yellow hydrants in the neighborhood belonged to the same water supply as the residential system. With the big fire in full force, many homes had collapsed or were destroyed, compromising the residential water supply. There was a secondary hydrant system that had black hydrants and were adjacent to the main road on Rockaway Point Boulevard. This system belonged to the city and was dedicated only to fire hydrants. Dufficy's plan was brilliant and we stretched to a nearby black hydrant and fed both hydrants into the pump. We now had good water pressure and it wasn't long before we extinguished the first fire of the night.

We were behind schedule and needed to get to the big fight. Again, the rulebook was out the window and instead of neatly folding the hose on the hose bed, we threw the lines loosely on the top of the truck. From a distance it looked like we had a delivery of spaghetti on our truck. Meanwhile, Mike Schramm completed his rescue of our senior citizen and found alternate transportation for him to safety. Mike jumped back on the truck, welcomed by his dogs happily wagging their tails. They were now perched on the center console totally attentive and feeling like they were a part of our team. Having been a dog owner, I knew that they had a keen sense of smell and could sense emotions like fear and conditions of danger. Their demeanor gave me confidence.

We now had to traverse the firestorm and the column of smoke again. This time it was easier because we had a proven method and we cleared most of the debris before-hand. We cleared the smoke plume to the east and were on our way to the Saint Thomas More church/public shelter when we saw a very alarming situation. As we passed by the Rockaway Point Volunteer firehouse, we could easily see their entire ap-paratus still in their firehouse and under water. The storm devastated all of their equipment and their mechanics were futilely trying to make them operational. This was really bad because we relied upon each other for backup. I didn't know if the Roxbury Fire Department suffered the same fate. Their firehouse was in a much greater protected area and they stood a good chance of getting their equipment running. Both of our trucks were operating, but I knew that at any point they could fail. Unit 7, "Big Jack," the new truck had many computer diodes and relays and unfor-tunately the manufacturer installed them underneath the main chassis. Most of them short circuited, causing a constant cacophony of bells and whistles. However, despite this mind-bending noise, the truck continued to operate. I again made a mental note in the event we were to order a new truck to place the delicate electronics higher up in a waterproof compartment. Later, when the story of the "Hail Mary" became known, our trucks were called the "Miracle Trucks of Breezy Point." Several months later a church group in Queens presented us with a painting of them in their glory.

We arrived at Saint Thomas More to a massive amount of chaos and confusion. People were all walking aimlessly and in an obvious state of shock. We off-loaded our survivors and attempted to disembark the dogs, though neither wanted to leave and they both defiantly maintained their position on the center console. They both saw themselves as full-fledged fire dogs and probably imagined themselves dressed with a Dalmatian pattern on their coat. It may have been a bad call, but I said the dogs had to go since I didn't want to expose them to any danger. Mike picked up one, who fought viciously, and I reached back from the front seat to give Maggie a nudge to follow. She took a nip at my hand and jumped out the door on the passenger side. She was upset and disappeared into the night. Mike futilely searched for her but to no avail. As a result, when it was time for us to leave Mike missed the truck. In hindsight I would have rather kept the dogs and have Mike as part of the team since I needed his strength and his experience. The dogs might have been safe inside the truck. It was a tough call. Hindsight is always 20-20 and at this point we didn't know what to expect during the night. Nearly a month later, through the miracle of the internet, Mike and Maggie reunited.

We proceeded to the northeast corner of the fire near the corner of 8th Avenue and 208th Street. The truck from Roxbury named "The Wild Thing" was already on scene as well as our Unit 7, "Big Jack." We now had three trucks to fight this monster plus members from the RPFD doing their best with hand tools trying to contain the advancement of the fire to the north.

Roxbury had a strainer device and was able to pump the standing water onto the fire. The strainer device was able to draw standing water and was able to screen most foreign objects from being sucked into the engine. Drafting is another way to get water on a fire. It is used mostly in rural areas and taps into water from static sources such as a lake or pond. The system has a hard suction line with a metal strainer designed to prevent debris from entering the pump systems. If the debris should enter the internal components of the pumps, they can damage the pump's impellor and disable the pump and ultimately the truck. Breezy Point at first glance, seems to be an ideal location for drafting water from the

Jamaica Bay to the north and the Atlantic Ocean to the south. It was the PBFD's experience many years ago that the drafting system didn't work. We found it to be dangerous and unreliable. We had bad luck with the strainer system because the strainer and filters were unable to completely keep out small objects like small beach shell fragments that could destroy the pump. The water surrounding the community was salt water and no matter how many times we flushed the system the long-term corrosive aspect of the salt water would also damage our pumps. We learned that the drafting process was unreliable. In our experience the pump would only last between twenty minutes to two hours using the strainer system and once you lose the pump you lose the truck. Therefore, as a policy we stayed away from using the strainer and would have to rely on the hydrant network. This was a decision made by our department long before my watch started. Roxbury was the first to put water on the big fire. They used the strainer.

Dufficy and I, with Sebastian Danese over my shoulder, quickly assessed the situation. With our limited manpower and equipment and after experiencing the fire jump to the northwest side of the community, we knew we had to get in front of the fire. The last thing I wanted to do was chase the fire, but we all knew it was important to get in front of it. The challenge was how to get there. I was growing impatient and wanted to move out right away. I really didn't want to traverse the smoke plume again because it was obviously very dangerous. So far, we were extremely lucky during our previous passages. There would be two routes if we chose to go further east to get to the southern perimeter along the Ocean Promenade. One would be Reid Avenue south to the Promenade or east along the "Sugar Bowl Express" to get to the Promenade. The locals gave it this name since it was the main road to everyone's favorite beach bar and candy store. Dufficy's critical thinking skills were in high gear. He didn't like the idea of going east and then south. He reminded me that the area to the east was not protected by sand dunes and that area may have been destroyed, making travel impossible and he was confident that we could get through the smoke plume and firestorm again without a problem. This was a critical decision. If we picked the wrong path and the truck became incapacitated, we would lose one third of the fire apparatus and there would be only two trucks remaining to fight the fire. All the roads were undermined and clogged with debris, so considering all that, we needed to pick the path with the greatest potential to get us to our intended position.

Dufficy's plan was to go west along Rockaway Beach Boulevard, then south down Beach 219th Street and finally turn east on Breezy Point Boulevard. If all went well, we would be positioned on the southwest corner of the fire. It would be a perfect position to stop the advance of the fire and try to prevent the fireballs from going airborne and incinerating the rest of the neighborhood. Dufficy's plan was risky but was our best option at the time. If his plan didn't work, we could always try the other as a backup. As a leader it is important to trust your team and listen to their input. I'm glad I did. Later we would find out that the roads from the southeast part of the property were totally blocked and impassable.

If our plan succeeded, there would be proper alignment among the fire departments. The RPFD would be guarding the northeast corner protecting the community of Rockaway Point and we would be positioned to guard the Breezy Point community on the west side. Roxbury and their truck "Wild Thing" would be available to back up both of us.

I made a radio call to Lieutenant Hernandez, the officer on Unit 7, Big Jack. "We're headed west on Rockaway Point Boulevard. We plan to take 219th Street south to Breezy Point Boulevard and position ourselves at the southwest corner of the fire. If we make it, I'll call you for backup."

He responded, "Roger, we'll prepare to move." We now had the seats in the back of Sand Flea filled with firefighters and I had extra men on the outside step holding onto whatever would support them. Dufficy steered through the black abyss streaked with its red fireballs down Rockaway Point Boulevard. No one had to tell any of us to take a large gulp of relatively fresh air before being smothered by the smoke ridden plume. Our method of using the rear spotlights and having Dufficy drive forward while looking backward was still working. As we travelled further west on Rockaway Beach Boulevard, we found new debris that needed to be removed. The firefighters dodged airborne material driven by the hurricane force winds, while clearing a path for the truck. When we emerged once again from the plume, we were near Beach 219th Street where we planned to travel south. We were shocked to see a mountain of debris blocking our path. This street is extra wide and is a main artery in this part of the community. Apparently when Sandy's tidal surge hit the peninsula, wide open areas like 219th Street acted as major causeways that helped the ocean meet the bay. The water moved with a velocity that helped to rip off wooden decks and anything else not completely secured. The access gate at the northern end of the street acted as a barrier that caused the flotsam to pile up over twenty feet high. We were momentarily stopped in our tracks as we assessed our current situation. It would be impossible to clear the area to open a path for the truck. Besides we would lose valuable time and the fire was still on the move. We quickly decided to see if Beach 220th Street was passable since it was a much narrower street and quite possibly had fewer obstructions. A cheer went up among our team when we turned the corner on Beach 220th Street to find a relatively open passageway. We raced to Breezy Point Boulevard and proceeded east again to enter the promenade. Dufficy's plan worked like a charm and we high fived each other. I was glad I listened to his plan. I radioed Big Jack and shared Dufficy's method of penetrating the smoke plume and the new route we discovered turning south on Beach 220th Street.

Firefighter Rick Savage was the chauffeur on Big Jack. His professional experience of snaking his big brown package truck through the traffic snarled streets of New York would come in handy. He followed Dufficy's method of penetrating the smoke plume and the route we discovered.

At the entrance to the promenade stood a metal boat trailer blocking our way. We were very close to the advancing fire and could hear the deafening sounds of crashing waves and wind to our south and the crackling of the fire just ahead. Our members dismounted and as they were picking up the trailer to clear the way, they had a close up and clear view of the monster we were soon to fight. We all shared an apprehensive look and I vaguely remember letting loose a string of curses. Once again, I asked if the FDNY had made it back to the peninsula. The answer came back negative and I told my crew we were on our own. I signed off, telling them we needed them ASAP because we were going in. My team heard every word and knew the risks they were being asked to take. Not one person hesitated. From the right front seat, I shouted the order to mount up and in my best attempt at understatement I shouted out, "We have a job to do."

Dufficy pulled up to the hydrant at the intersection of Gotham Walk and the promenade. As we dismounted from the truck, we stood there in awe and assessed the situation. Our past training prepared us to be aware of some of the hidden hazards and threats but nothing would ever fully prepare us for what we were now experiencing. The sand lanes were covered with water and we knew underneath the sand and debris were the two threats of cesspools and sink holes. The community does not have sewers and uses septic tanks and cesspools. The entire neighborhood was honeycombed with hundreds of six to eight feet deep septic wells that would hold the effluent from the homes. The fast-floodwaters could have easily uncovered and removed a cesspool cover exposing a six-foot-deep death trap. A sink hole was different and potentially more dangerous. Sink holes were originally blow holes and were created when the flood initially happened. Besides having the ocean race to meet the bay, the water table which normally resides eight to ten feet below the sandy surface becomes flooded and is forced to the surface. Water typically seeks the path of least resistance. Later, we had reports of people witnessing geyser-like eruptions of water shooting six feet in the air. After the flooding, when the water was receding it would return in the same path, causing a sink hole. The sand adjacent to the sink hole became liquefied like quicksand and when the water finished returning to the water table the sink hole collapsed and the surrounding liquefied sand backfilled the hole, burying anything in its path. No one knew how deep a sink hole went but we estimated them to be much deeper than a cesspool. Both were very dangerous because they were impossible to see and with our heavy bunker gear we could drown or be buried alive in the attempt to extricate ourselves. Fortunately, we were trained to use the buddy system and keep an eye on each other. If we didn't back each other up, a brother could disappear without anyone knowing. We debated which would be the worst death: a cesspool or a sink hole. Despite the malodorous and unsanitary conditions of a cesspool, we all would have preferred falling into a cesspool instead of being buried alive in a sink hole.

The fire was huge and the combination of fifty-foot flames made depth perception impossible. It looked like the whole neighborhood was on fire. Besides the unseen hazards there were many other threats to be evaluated. Most homes had a gas barbeque grill fueled by propane tanks and we could hear them exploding. The fire to the north crossed into the parking lot and cars were aflame with their gas tanks exploding as well. The entire area was like a battlefield. Everything was on fire, including the electrical wires between the utility poles. Parts of some houses were still standing but fully engulfed, and as debris broke loose from the dying structures the embers would become airborne by the hurricane force winds and fly into the smoke plume. The power lines connecting the homes, ablaze with red flames, looked like some crisscrossed red ruby necklace. Not knowing the status of the power grid, we treated each wire as a live wire to avoid electrocution.

We were at the origin of the smoke plume. The fire was so massive that it was creating its own local weather pattern. Later we learned that FDNY declared this a six-alarm fire and when the fire was totally extinguished the final count was sadly the loss of 135 homes. This was one of the largest residential fires in the history of the City of New York.

Initially the hydrant hook ups went well. We stretched hoses up the sand lane between Hudson and Gotham Walks. We unpacked the spaghetti packed hose first and then used more from the hose bed. The wind was on our backs blowing the heat and smoke away from us so we were able to push north to the third and fourth house from the foot of Hudson Walk. Homes on both sides of us and all homes to the front were ablaze, creating a cave of fire where the fifty-foot flames were to the right, left, overhead and in front of us. If the wind shifted, we would all be in grave danger. If the wall of fire collapsed, our plan was to make a run for it to the south. It was not a good plan because the Atlantic Ocean was right behind us with its threatening waves. If the wind changed there was really no place to go. There wasn't any good plan, we just hoped for the best.

The quiet and calm inside the "grotto of fire" made the whole environment surreal. The young firefighters asked how we should start the attack and it was probably poor timing, but I came back with a new animal metaphor. I asked them how one eats an elephant. They looked at me with surprise and were not able to come up with an answer. I said to them, "One bite at a time." Instantly they all knew what I meant. I pointed to the back of a house to our immediate west on Hudson Walk, "Let's start here and do our best to stop the westward advancement." I also formed a squad of firefighters to use their pike poles and tools to knock down some of the standing structures that were fully ablaze. I wanted to stop the never-ending supply line of hot flying embers that were making the smoke plume very dangerous. These airborne embers were a real threat and most likely caused the fire to jump to the northeast side of the property.

Initially, all seemed to be working well. Rick Savage successfully navigated "BIG JACK" through the blinding smoke plume and pulled up behind us at the end of Irving Walk, and all of my men were in the same place again. It wasn't long before we realized we had water pressure problems. We were hooked up to a yellow hydrant and encountered the same problem we had on our first fire. The black hydrants were a quarter of a mile to the north and it was impossible to drag the hoses through the fire. Dufficy made the decision to stretch to another hydrant further east at the juncture of Ocean Avenue and the promenade. Our initial plan was to have both hydrants feed into our pumper and hopefully we could build up enough pressure to fight the fire. The backup plan was to have "Big Jack" hook up to a hydrant and then feed yet another line into the "Sand Flea's" pump. The problem was that we were connected to the same water line and it was like putting two or three straws into an empty glass and still hoping to draw more fluids. Our least attractive back up plan was to shut down the nozzle to let the pressure build up. At the right time we would then open up the line till the pressure dissipated once again. It was a dangerous plan and none of us liked it.

At one point I was dragging some extra hoses through the flood waters so that we could go further north into the fire zone. I was in the sand lane on the southwest corner of Gotham Walk when everything went bad. Fortunately, I had my hands on the hose line because I suddenly found myself in water over my head clinging on for dear life. I had apparently stepped into either an uncovered cesspool or a sink hole. Since I didn't smell any funky odors and couldn't find the bottom with my feet, I was pretty certain I was in a sink hole. Within seconds the two O'Brien brothers and their father were working to extricate me. My bunker pants and boots were starting to fill up with sand and water pulling me down. Had it not been for the quick actions of the O'Brien family my role as chief might have ended quickly. While recovering from my brush with death on the back step of our truck, I remembered being a little out of sorts earlier in the evening when the nice elderly lady in the clubhouse failed to return my bunker coat. Had she returned it and I was wearing it when I went for a swim in the sinkhole, the extra weight would have been deadly. I am a firm believer that there are no coincidences and that everything happens for a reason.

I was totally soaked and the water was freezing. My radio was no longer working and my wet clothing was draining my body temperature. I found my way back into the cave of fire and let the heat help dry my clothes and restore my body temperature. I profusely thanked the O'Brien family and put out the word to be on the lookout for sinkholes and to make sure we backed each other up. The process of shutting down the nozzle and allowing the pressure to build up was slow going. There was still a great amount of standing water in the area. I asked the men to be on the lookout for any five-gallon plastic buckets. In the old days, before pumpers, firefighters would fight fires with buckets, hence the term "bucket brigade." As a last-ditch effort, I wanted to start a bucket brigade and continue the fight, but we couldn't find any. We continued to fight the fire by allowing the water pressure to rebuild and concentrated our efforts on stopping any fire embers from going airborne.

At around 11:30 pm, I saw three civilians walking west-bound on the promenade and turning north on Gotham Walk. During some other hurricane events the local bar was known to have 'hurricane parties' where the patrons defied the evacuation orders and chose instead to remain and celebrate for whatever reason. My initial thoughts were that these three people were sightseers fresh out of the bar. Not wanting them to complicate our fire zone, I approached them with the intent to keep them out. When I got close, I recognized them. They weren't sightseers from the local bar but rather seasoned off duty FDNY firefighters and two of them were brothers. The brothers grew up on Gotham Walk and came down to witness the horror firsthand and to help where they could. Both were in total awe of the situation. We were next to a house on the east side of the block that was collapsing onto a house that was now being ignited by the dying structure. One of the brothers turned to me and said, "It's a shame. That house belongs to the widow of a victim from the 9/11 attacks. It looks like it's totaled."

The house had to contain many important memories. I knew the story of her husband's death and how she came to own the house. The three friends left the area shortly and continued their survey. I turned to Firefighter Mike Scotko and said to him, "Do what you can to save this house. There is an important story here."

I returned to the area twenty minutes later and the men had pulled the collapsing wall engulfed in flames away from the widow's house and were doing their best to wet down the house to prevent it from being engulfed in flames. I was standing on the front deck and fire was everywhere. Even right underneath me flames were coming up from below the deck. It was a long night and I had to urinate badly. Not wanting to waste any efforts, I urinated on the flames flickering up through the decking. It actually worked but smelt horrible. I noticed that my urine was a dark yellow almost brown, a sign I was becoming dehydrated. As the night wore on, I would find out firsthand the impact of becoming dehydrated. I made a mental note to put cases of water on each truck to keep the firefighters hydrated.

The men were exhausted and we started rotating crews and taking breaks. About 1:00 am, I was at the front of our position in the sand lane between Hudson and Gotham Walks when I started to notice a red shape like a firetruck in the red blur of the fire. On a closer look, we could see an amorphous line of firetrucks across the battlefield with hoses pushing out a considerable amount of pressure. I felt like I was lost in a desert staring at a mirage in hopes of a rescue. In disbelief, I yelled over to one of our firefighters and asked, "Are you seeing what I'm seeing?"

His exhausted face blackened with soot and grime came alive and all of us started shouting with joy. The cavalry, in the shape of the FDNY, had arrived and it was apparent that they were getting their water from the black hydrants a quarter of a mile away. They had the resources, equipment, people and the water pressure. Life was getting better now that we were no longer alone. They had several ladder trucks with the ladder extended horizontally with a firefighter and a nozzle at the end. They were deeply penetrating the belly of the fire beast. From where I was standing the fire was starting to come under control.

Once the FDNY is on scene they become the incident commander and we work with them. During the night and well prior to our standdown, a chief from the task force found his way to our location. We met briefly and I explained what we were doing. He thanked us and said to keep doing what we were doing. If they were unhappy with our performance, they could in theory take over our equipment. Our relationship with the FDNY has always been extremely healthy.

At 5:00 am, with dawn approaching, our entire department was totally exhausted. We stayed out all night hooting with the owls and we flew like eagles. I was very proud of them, and notified the FDNY that the PBFD was standing down. I ordered my men to pack up our gear and to find a place to rest. We knew our firehouse was destroyed and we couldn't use it without a great deal of work. Someone offered the Catholic Club and said they had some dry beds with a place to sleep. "Ok, let's go there."

Big Jack was the first truck to arrive at the Catholic Club. It was the building next to the RPFD whose trucks were knocked out by the initial flood. A grim reminder of how the night could have gone for us.

We learned that the FDNY was fighting several fires on the peninsula. Belle Harbor had a two-alarm fire in the vicinity of Beach 130th Street and there was another multi-dwelling fire on Rockaway Beach Boulevard and Beach 115th Street. We were lucky because the incident commander of FDNY Task Force, Chief Joe Pfeifer came from Rockaway Point and knew the local neighborhood. He started out as a teenage volunteer firefighter in the Rockaway Point Fire Department (RPFD). Based upon reports he received on his way to the scene, he elevated the fire quickly to a six-alarm fire and was able to get enough equipment in a short amount of time. This was a great decision. They arrived sometime after midnight when the flood waters were still high and hurricane force winds were still in force. They lost many trucks to the flood waters but despite the odds they found a way to bring the necessary resources to fight each of the three fires. The whole city was under siege with floods and fires in Staten Island and in Red Hook, Brooklyn. Later we found out that the major Con Ed power plant in lower Manhattan exploded. Chief Pfeifer gave the order to the utility companies to shut down, saving many hundreds of homes. Chief Pfeifer was also the first battalion chief on scene on 9/11/2001 and he knew his business. We were extraordinarily lucky to have him. He retired in July 2018.

I was still on the "Sand Flea" on our return trip. Our exit route followed the same roadways we used to get in. Along the way we passed a line of about twenty FDNY fire trucks fully staffed and ready to go. They apparently were a secondary line of defense in case the fire jumped. The FDNY had trained their leaders well and their chiefs had laid out a military style of assault. In war, besides the heroics of brave troops, the battles are really won by managing logistics. In a fire battle when it looks like the job is winding down, some set of unfortunate circumstances could cause a flare up equal to or exceeding the intensity of the fire at its worst. FDNY's philosophy of having fresh firefighters at the ready in a nearby location was brilliant.

We passed the area where the blinding smoke plume and firestorm was at its strongest and there was no evidence it even existed. The best I could tell, the only time the fire jumped was when we found the house on Bayway Walk on fire. Now the big question that must be answered was, "Did anyone in Breezy die because of Sandy?" My team searched the collapsed homes and we hadn't found any victims. Later in the day the NYPD did an expanded house-to-house search to determine if there were any victims.

On our drive to our new quarters, we found some stragglers who were sloshing through the standing water and picked them up to bring them to the public shelter at Saint Thomas More Church. I was totally exhausted and knew I was in trouble. My clothes were still soaked and now that I was out of the fire, my wet clothes were sapping my body heat. Hypothermia was starting to set in. We arrived at the church and I assisted in off-loading the survivors. It was when I raised my right leg, the three feet to the step, to get back into the truck that my right hamstring muscle started to spasm and then lock up. It was a hellacious crippling pain and I didn't want the young guys to know that I was hurting. Since our plan was to search the neighborhood for other stragglers and bring them to the shelter, they were yelling for me to get back on the truck. My stubborn Irish personality kicked in when I told them to calm down. I tried using my left leg on the elevated step and I grabbed onto the hand holds to pull myself into the truck when my left hamstring muscle started to spasm again and then locked up. I immediately collapsed and fell to the ground and groaned loudly in pain. I thought back to earlier in the evening when I pissed on the fire the yellowish-brownish color of my urine and by now I was severely dehydrated as well as facing the early stages of hypothermia.

Both the chauffeur, Tim Dufficy, and Firefighter Mike Scotko came to my assistance. They tried to get me into the truck but my legs only gave me more pain. They were anxious to get going to search the area for more survivors. I told them to get back to the truck and be on their way. They refused and asked what I was going to do. I said, "If necessary, I'll crawl into the church and try to let my legs get some rest so that they'll start working again."

They didn't agree and insisted that they carry me into the church. They placed my arms around their shoulders and carried me with my lifeless legs dragging behind. I must have looked like a disabled person going to church in search of a miracle. The church was darkened with just a few flashlights flickering about. Like everything else in the community, the church was flooded and still had some standing water. The heat system had failed and besides being damp, it was cold. People in the church were all huddled trying to survive. Many were silently praying.

Scotko and Dufficy got me through the lobby and fortunately found the first half of the right rear pew was open. They laid me out there and said they would check on me later. My head was to the center of the pew with my feet at the center aisle. I tried my best to be absolutely still to stop the leg spasms but my body was so cold that the shivering would set off a new round of leg spasms. In the Air Force, I attended cold weather survivor school and learned that the shivering response was a good sign. When a person who was suffering from hypothermia stopped the shivering response, it meant that the body's core temperature was falling too low and death could be imminent, therefore I was happy to be shivering. I also knew that the combination of hypothermia and dehydration could cause my thinking to become distorted. I needed to find a way to get dry clothes and some water. The best place to go would be my house but I didn't know if it survived the fire and storm. In my house I had a great collection of vitamins and health aides including a supply of potassium pills that would help stop the cramping. I also had bottles of water and dry clothes. My priority was to find a way to get back to my house.

I used the rigid oak pew to help straighten my legs and to calm the muscle spasms. The shivering effect continued my rocking, rolling and groaning in pain. I felt if I died there, it wouldn't be far to travel to have a Requiem Mass. In the Air Force, I rescued survivors from a sunken fishing vessel off Long Island. It was January and the Atlantic was freezing. They were in the advanced stages of hypothermia and besides dry woolen blankets, we used our crewmembers to wrap themselves next to the victims, to share body heat.

As I was trying to develop my plan, I heard a voice over my shoulder. Out of the darkness I recognized her voice and realized it was my 85-year-old neighbor, Elaine Smith. I was good friends with her, her daughter and son for over 50 years. She also had a white Labrador Retriever named "Champagne" that I would meet whenever she was on one of her walks. In her best understatement Elaine asked, "And how are you doing today, Marty?"

Being in a state of denial I responded, "I'm doing fine. How are you?" It was an absurd conversation since we were both in surroundings ravaged by the disaster that we just experienced. I began to hear rustling on her other side and realized that Champagne was next to her. In addition, her daughter, Mary Elizabeth was hibernating in the pew in front of us.

I was seriously considering telling Elaine about my hypothermia and wanted to see if I could borrow Champagne to trade body heat. Before I had a chance to make my request, Firefighter Rick Savage, Chauffer of "Big Jack," came in to see if I was OK. I felt like my legs were gaining strength and I asked Rick to help me into the truck. I bade farewell to Elaine and her daughter and they asked if we could come back and give them a lift to their house. I left thinking how hard my guardian angel was working for me and for them.

It was now daylight, and as we turned the corner, I could see that my house was still there. As I looked around, I could see first-hand the devastation that rained down on our neighborhood. The fire zone was huge and still smoldering. The whole place looked like a bombed-out city in Europe in the midst of World War II. It would be a miracle if no one died. Rick waited while I ran into my house only to see everything destroyed. There were even mussels and other shells from the ocean in my kitchen sink. I found some dry clothes in the upper reaches of my closet and some bottled water untouched by the floodwaters. I swallowed a potassium pill and some other vitamins and felt like a new man. I was ready to go back to work.

The miracle trucks of PBFD in front of St. Thomas More Church, which acted as a public shelter site the night of the storm.

CHAPTER 8

The Immediate Aftermath

POLICE OFFICER'S CREED

*As a law enforcement officer, my fundamental duty
is to serve mankind; to safeguard
lives and property, to protect the innocent
against deception, the –weak against
oppression or intimidation, and the peaceful
against violence or disorder; and to respect
the Constitutional rights of all men to
liberty, equality, and justice.*

*I-will keep my private life unsullied
as an example to all, maintain courageous calm in
the face of danger, scorn, or ridicule;
develop self-restraint; and be constantly mindful
of the welfare of others. Honest in thought
and deed in both my personal and official
life, I will be exemplary in obeying the laws
of the land and the regulations of my
department. Whatever I see or hear of a
confidential nature or that is confided to me in
my official capacity – will be kept ever secret
unless revelation is necessary in the
performance of my duty.*

*I will never act officiously or permit
personal feelings, prejudices, animosities, or
friendships to influence my decisions.
With no compromise for crime and with relentless
prosecution of criminals, I-will enforce
the law courteously and appropriately without
fear or favor, malice or ill will, never
employing unnecessary force or
violence and never
accepting gratuities.*

THE TRANSITION FROM the fire to the recovery was almost seamless. Rick turned Big Jack around and we returned to Saint Thomas More to pick up Champagne, Mary Elizabeth and her Mom. We dropped them off at their home and watched them as they began their own journey to restore order out of chaos. There was an eerie silence as we patrolled the area, assessing the damage and looking for survivors. We were also looking for those who might not have survived. During the night, I lost my phone and was unable to communicate with my family. My wife wisely evacuated to stay with good friends, the McEwen's, who lived on Long Island. Trish and George both spent their summers in Breezy Point, and Trish's mom still owned a house and was spending her retirement years living full time in Breezy Point. She evacuated as well and spent the night in New Jersey with her daughter, Lorie. I found a phone and called my wife to tell her I was OK. Trish answered and almost immediately asked me how her mother's house was. There was a dreadful and prolonged silence as I was searching to find the most delicate words that would let her know that the entire house was gone. Finally, I told her that it was destroyed and that nothing was left. It was like telling someone that a family member had died.

Trish was in shock and gave the phone to my wife. My wife was happy that I was OK but couldn't understand why I didn't call her sooner. I explained how the phone was destroyed after the sink hole. I didn't tell her of my night of survival in the back of the church. She had sent our son, MJ, and Trish's son, Mike McEwen to look for me. Both were FDNY firefighters. I looked forward to their arrival and had plans to use their skills since we had a serious manpower shortage. With the exception of Rick and me, the entire department was in crew rest in the back of the Catholic Club. They were all totally exhausted. The radio calls for help started to come in. At one point we had two serious calls at the same time which would require both of our trucks. One was a middle-aged man with stage four throat cancer. He was unable to speak due to his cancer and couldn't ask for help. He spent the night alone in his house. When the floodwaters invaded his house, he climbed on top of his dresser. His neighbor found him there the following morning and called for our assistance. He was in need of immediate medical attention and required transport to a hospital. We were called to respond rather than the FDNY because we had the four-wheel drive vehicle and we knew how to navigate about the debris-laden neighborhood. The emergency notification system was in disarray and we received the call from local people using their cell phones.

The other call was for an exploding transformer that required us to secure the area till the utility company arrived. I had the unpleasant job of trying to wake Lieutenant Kevin Hernandez who was resting peacefully in the back of the Catholic Club. The conversation didn't go well until he fully woke up and I explained that we were the only game in town. The FDNY had not yet set up their Disaster Assistance Center in Breezy and were swamped by emergency calls throughout the city. The RPFD did not have operational trucks that could operate in the flooded areas and the FDNY equipment returned to their quarters.

I told Kevin he could take the transformer job with the Sand Flea and Rick and I would take Big Jack to rescue the cancer patient. On the way to pick up the patient, I saw my son MJ and his friend Mike and told them I needed their help. They jumped on board and we went to Beach 220th Street for the transport. I had known Mike McEwen all of his life and he was like another son to me. Despite exhaustion, I was proud and honored to be working a job with these two young men. MJ and Mike took the patient off the dresser and carried him into the back seat of "Big Jack." He was seated between MJ and Mike who looked like giants guarding their patient. He had this broad grin on his face and was enjoying the moment. I turned and asked him if this was his first ride in a firetruck, and he nodded his head in the affirmative and silently gave us a thumbs up, indicating he thought it was cool. We transferred him to a police utility truck which brought him to the hospital. Thanks to the combined efforts of the three volunteer fire departments and the FDNY, no one died in Breezy Point from Hurricane Sandy.

MJ and Mike headed to Long Island for some fresh clothing and a hot shower. Mike's pick-up truck was trapped in the flood waters inundating the Broad Channel community and his truck would later be determined to be unsalvageable. MJ and Mike rescued several people during the storm and the following morning. Their off-duty exploits would have qualified them for recognition from the FDNY. They never submitted the paperwork and said they were only doing their job.

Sandy's devastation continued. Because of the busy firehouse activity in advance of the storm I never had a chance to reposition my personal car to high ground. It was also destroyed. Around 10:00 am, except for a small squad, I directed our team to go into crew rest. At 2:00 pm we would meet at our firehouse to make an assessment of our present situation, and develop a plan to adapt to our new situation. Most of the team went back to the Catholic Club. I went to my house and took in the damage now visible in the full sunlight. The lower end of the bed sheets in my bedroom were touching the water and the wetness was wicking up moisture to the entire bed. I chose to be away from the team because I knew that for many years I'd had a snoring problem. Had I bunked with the team they would not have received any rest, and I would be the butt of their jokes. I am certain they really didn't want the chief to be constantly around and needed some time to let their hair down and relax. I immediately fell into a deep sleep until around 1:00 pm, when I was rudely awakened by some loud knocking on my front door. It was a NYPD Officer doing a body count to see if everyone was accounted for. We talked a little before he went on his way and I was elated to hear that so far no one had died.

At 2:00 pm our team assembled at the firehouse and as a group we walked over to the fire zone. It was less than ten hours since we packed up our equipment and left the battleground. Embers were still smoldering and we could see blue flames spewing from severed gas lines once connected to household stoves and gas heaters. The area was totally devastated. One person found an American flag and had it proudly standing next to some of the debris. At the north end of Gotham Walk there was a statue of the Blessed Mother in a half shell. The half shell looked like a clam shell. Because we lived in a beach community it was easy to respectfully develop the nickname, the Clam Shell Mary Statue. It had been there for years next to the house. Now the house was in smoldering ruins but miraculously the statue looked like it was untouched except for some soot. We felt a special connection to the statue and remembered how Steve Glavey led our survivors in a 'prayer huddle' saying the "Hail Mary." The undamaged statue was like a calling card to tell us she was with us during the night. Many months later, I asked Steve why he switched to the "Hail Mary" after I said the two "Our Fathers" which thus far seemed to have been getting positive results. I wasn't unhappy and I thought it was a nice change to invoke the Blessed Mother. Our Miracle Trucks of Breezy Point were living proof. He told me when he was in Catholic grammar school a nun asked him to say the "Our Father" in front of the class. He said he botched it so bad that the nun gave him a royal tirade at the end. He knew he could do a better job saying the "Hail Mary." Steve was 65 years old when he led our prayer huddle in the "Hail Mary." It was nearly sixty years earlier that he received the rebuke from the nun for saying the "Our Father" improperly. He still remembered. Either way our prayers were heard and our operating trucks were living proof.

As I walked in the smoldering ruins, I couldn't help wondering why we were so unlucky to have this happen. The storm was well off-shore and only when it was near the New York area, did it choose to make a left turn. It was the only place on the east coast where the

This untouched statue surived the surrounding destruction.

shoreline twists at a ninety-degree angle. The area it hit represented some of the most densely populated areas in the entire United States.

The conversations among the firefighters during this walking tour recalled the events of the previous evening and the men began using biblical metaphors to describe our experiences. They described the flood as being of biblical proportions and referred to the Genesis flood where Noah built his Ark to save a portion of humanity from the disaster. They also described the fire as being of apocalyptic proportions as described in the Bible when referring to the Last Judgment Day.

I struggled, wondering whether this twin disaster was a result of God's wrath or was a natural phenomenon. Some of my atheistic and agnostic friends would say that an all-powerful and loving God would not allow something like this to happen; therefore, He does not exist or they choose not to believe in Him. I knew that, globally, disasters are prevalent. I began to reject the notion that this event was a result of divine retribution or something that God would prevent. Didn't we see the night before, after each "prayer huddle" our prayers were answered? As a pilot, I knew the science of meteorology could explain the development of a superstorm. The European Center for Medium Range Weather Forecasting predicted it would turn in the direction of New York.

I knew that this disaster would cause many people to pause and re-evaluate their lives. I concluded that these disasters were natural occurrences. Sadly, bad things happen to good people when, by coincidence, they are innocently in the path of some powerful force of nature. Superstorms are "equal opportunity disruptors" and they equally impact the good and bad. Even insurance companies when they wrote their policies addressed "acts of God." They describe an act of God as an event outside of human control or activity. Insurance policies usually specify which acts of God they cover. These clauses typically limit or remove liability for injuries, damages or losses caused by acts of God.

On a positive note, I also saw that despite the death and destruction these storms brought with them, they also brought heavy rains that replenished dangerously low water reservoirs and other areas impacted by drought conditions.

While these storms would cause many to re-evaluate their lives, many others would use these events to extend help and kindness to those in need. It would be an opportunity to exhibit the best side of humanity. While we toured the new fire zone, I made a conscious decision to reach out to the best side of humanity and invite them to come to our aid. Tim Dufficy and Seabass used social media to contact other volunteer fire departments around the country to solicit their help. The response was huge.

We were at the center of the fire zone and were approached by a reporter from a major newspaper. Many of us were wearing our turn out gear from the night before. It was not hard to figure out that we were members of the PBFD. He started to ask some questions and initially we were reluctant to participate in an interview. In my career with the FAA, I was trained as a senior manager to work with the press. I called the team together to emphasize the importance of us telling our story. It was a good story, and if we didn't take the time to tell it, others might inaccurately create their own. I knew that in big organizations contact with the media was limited to a public-affairs officer or a representative of upper management. I also knew that each one of us had our own story to tell. Each perspective would not be just about fighting a monster fire inside of a flood and hurricane but it would be about Sandy's impact upon them, their community, and their family's lives. This was an important decision. Our story was really the story of all firefighters throughout the country and around the world and it needed to be told by them. There was an inner team within the firehouse that I referred to as "the core group." They were friends with each other both within and outside of the firehouse. During Superstorm Sandy they became the heart and soul of our organization. As their chief, I learned they were highly capable in many areas and not just firefighting. I knew I could rely upon them in many ways. Each member of the core group was intelligent and after watching some interviews they became confident enough to interact with the press individually.

Personally, I wanted to brag about the core group and the outstanding job they did. I wanted to tell the story of how they rescued me out of the sink hole and later when they again rescued me after I collapsed in front of the church. Most importantly, I wanted to tell the story of how they prevented the spread of the fire and prevented two thousand homes from being incinerated.

We found our way back to the firehouse and started to assess the damage. My heart was broken because everything was a wreck. The cabinets that Marty Walsh once repaired and the plumbing fixed by Ricky Savage were destroyed. The beverage cans and empty Guinness bottles that we were saving for the Department's morale fund were scattered everywhere. It looked like we had one hell of a party. The flood waters left a residue that contaminated everything it came into contact with. Our cots and sleeping materials were in tatters and the remnants of our turkey dinner that we never consumed were strewn all over the place. The sad truth was that our firehouse was not fit for human habitation.

Several of the young firemen were showing outstanding situational leadership skills. I turned to Tim Dufficy, who was a wizard with the internet and social media. He already knew I was a dinosaur when it came to technology. Our request for assistance from other volunteer fire departments was spot on. Many of our members had either totally lost their homes to the fire and flood or they needed many hours of work to make their homes livable. This was another important decision because we recognized early on that we couldn't do this alone. I also asked Tim if he could rehabilitate our web page for the PBFD and chronicle and document our journey. Sebastian Danese and Kevin Hernandez also came in with some great ideas. We knew the firehouse was uninhabitable. We had an emergency generator that was elevated, but not high enough for the record-breaking flood waters of Hurricane Sandy. It became unusable shortly after Hurricane Sandy's floodwaters hit the peninsula. Besides having no electricity, we did not have any running water or sanitation, so we used an abandoned five-gallon bucket and lined it with a contractor waste bag that was preserved until garbage removal would be re-initiated. It was a start. The floodwaters that invaded the firehouse left moisture inside the walls. This moisture began to wick upward through the insulation. Mold, mildew and an unhealthy smell permeated the entire building. Flotsam was everywhere and the aforementioned slimy residue was an issue. The makeup of this slime was unknown and probably bordering on some kind of hazardous material. I knew when it dried it would turn into a dust which would later become airborne. I didn't want anyone to get sick, so we had to find a temporary place to serve as our firehouse.

In addition, besides having to find a new firehouse we had to get some emergency maintenance done to our trucks. In essence we had to rebuild everything in the department from the ground up. Despite the fact that we were in the shadow of the New York City skyline our piece of the world quickly became less than a developing Third World country.

CHAPTER 9

My Fears

"WE WANT TO know what happened." The stern voice came from the lead FDNY Fire Marshal. When we returned from our inspection of the fire zone, there were two fire marshals waiting for us in our back room and they didn't look happy. The fire marshals are like the criminal investigators of the fire department. They carry a badge and a gun and they have arrest authority. They are law enforcement officers.

The pair divided their roles of being a "good cop" and "bad cop." Right now, their presence was intimidating. I didn't know how this meeting was going to go and directed our extra firefighters to leave the room so that we had a level of privacy. There was a significant amount of work all over the place and I didn't need an audience. Besides, I knew that with the fatigue, the core group would not be open to any criticism and I was concerned that things could escalate. I asked Tim Dufficy to join me for the meeting. He had a good head on his shoulders and constantly demonstrated good judgment during the entire night.

I found four relatively dry chairs amidst the wreckage of the back room. All of us ignored the noxious odors emanating from the restrooms and the smells from our untouched rotting turkey dinner. We sat down, surrounded by the debris, including hundreds of recyclable Guinness beer bottles scattered about the room. In addition to the odors, the air was frosty and charged with tension. Truthfully there was not any good place to have this meeting. My healthy paranoia was kicking in, and I was wondering why this meeting was occurring so quickly. I now knew that our fire was a six alarm and there were two other big fires in Rockaway, only five miles away. Word was filtering in that some people were fatally injured in the Rockaway fires. The FDNY had evacuated their personnel and equipment on the Peninsula in advance of the hurricane and had significant problems getting back when the fires broke out. I was fearful that somehow they would judge that we acted inappropriately.

The questions came hot and heavy, giving me the impression that this was not an interview but rather an inquisition. With a grim face, the lead investigator asked, "In your own words tell us what happened." I explained the conscious decision we made to remain at our quarters and shelter in place despite the Mayor's order to evacuate the peninsula. "Our decision not to evacuate and abandon our station was made because we knew this was our place to be, and we couldn't leave the community unguarded." Both Tim and I described the need to abandon the firehouse during the flood and re-establish ourselves in the clubhouse. We informed them how we became an impromptu public shelter for over forty survivors, and we covered how we wrestled with the decision to evacuate the clubhouse during the rising flood waters. We shared how we had the "prayer huddles" and described the necessary decision to evacuate during the firestorm.

We also shared the story of how, during the evacuation, we diverted to the northwest side of the property to rescue an elderly man, only to discover that the fire jumped nearly a quarter of a mile. I explained that one house was fully engulfed and threatening all of the homes downwind of the location. This part seemed to interest them the most. They had already reviewed all of the radio calls from the night before yet didn't know anything about this situation. They heavily grilled us on whether or not we called the fire in to dispatch. Duffity was on top of it and convinced them that he made the call. Apparently, if we didn't make the call, we would have been the

PBFD back room meetings

recipients of some sort of disciplinary action. The meeting lasted for over two hours. It was the first time to tell our story. I told them how for nearly two days we spent every waking moment developing plans, changing them and finding new and innovative ways to guarantee our own survival as well as the community's continued existence. We had a short break in reacting to our environment and were able to report on our actions to find order out of chaos. Sadly, it would be a short break with nearly a year's worth of chaos ahead. Toward the end of the meeting, I noticed the stone-faced mask seemed to soften. Finally, when it seemed like the inquisition was over, I asked the lead investigator, "What should we expect as an outcome of this meeting? Specifically, should we expect any disciplinary action?"

The stone face on the fire marshal completely faded and he said, "I don't think you have anything to worry about. From the way my partner and I see it, you and your department are heroes." Shying away from that particular praise and believing that the only day any of us were true heroes was the day we took the oath of office to become a fireman, I responded by saying, "We were only doing our job." It was the first time we were called heroes and it made me uncomfortable. Unknown to us then, there would be many other times we would hear that salutation. I felt the tears of relief and joy welling up in my eyes and as I looked at the three others, I saw they were reacting in the same way. My earlier feeling of "healthy paranoia" was once again proven to be unjustified.

As the meeting broke up, the lead investigator nonchalantly dropped a big bomb on me that was going to cause me to lose sleep over the next couple of months. He said, "You know you have a big problem on your hands. After Hurricane Katrina hit New Orleans, it became common knowledge that a separate flood insurance policy from their homeowner's insurance policy was needed. Suddenly, there was a rash of mysterious house fires in the area."

If they were quietly whispering this threat to us, I was certain that law enforcement agencies and insurance companies across the country were on high alert to this type of nefarious activity. With the advancement of forensic tools and the sophistication of the well-trained arson investigator, a person would be making a big mistake to get involved in such a criminal activity.

I had just experienced the worst night of my life and this revelation wasn't helping to make things any better. My initial response was in defense of the community. "This is a faith-based community and before the storm these people generously gave their money and other good deeds to help strangers in distress and to help each other. No one in their right mind would do such an act and jeopardize the entire neighborhood. These people are not only my neighbors but they are like extended family."

He responded, "It will only take one greedy person. You need to have a plan and stay alert." He and his partner quietly left our devastated firehouse and stepped into our newly shattered world. If they quietly whispered this threat to us, I was sure that our local security and law enforcement would also be informed. The fire marshals were right and we needed to develop a plan to be on alert and be able to respond.

I turned to Dufficy and he agreed that the residents of Breezy would not become arsonists, no matter what kind of bind they are in with their insurance companies but we also both knew we needed to have a plan just in case that one desperate person stooped to commit a crime of arson and insurance fraud.

In the past, we relied upon our residents to call in any fires to our security booth, which in turn activated the sirens to call the volunteers. Right now, the community was without any residents to call in a fire and without electricity the sirens were inoperable. In addition, the community's sand lanes were not passable. Most of the sand lanes contained collapsed septic tanks and storm debris which made the sand lanes unpassable to any vehicle. Our hydrant system was also collapsed and most likely unusable. In a neighborhood devoid of people, it would be easy for a person to come in and torch their own home under the cover of darkness. We had a skeleton crew from our own small private security force that did patrol the area but it was a large area. With no one in the area to sound the distress call for help and with no power or phone lines, the fire could spread rapidly and once again we could be at high risk for losing the entire neighborhood. Dufficy and I agreed not to repeat this warning. If we did, the word could spread and give some negative ideas to people looking for a way to recover on their homeowner's policy. It could become a self-fulfilling prophecy. Thus, it would be our secret and our constant worry.

Developing an arson response plan was one of the many contingencies we needed to consider. This came at a time when we were flat on our backs. All of our members' homes were either heavily damaged or destroyed. One of my cars was destroyed as well as the chief's utility vehicle. Many of our volunteer firefighters were re-locating away from the community out of necessity. I needed a trained and qualified team of firefighters with immediate availability to handle any emergency whether it be a natural or man-made event.

Besides the imminent threat of arson, I also had another fear that I couldn't share with anyone. I had a fear that another hurricane would strike before year's end. No one was ready for a repeat performance and we were extremely vulnerable. If it did strike, I was certain that many people would not have the will to rebuild.

I had a long and varied history with hurricanes. In 1960, I was ten years old and protected my sister and mother when Hurricane Donna struck us in Breezy Point. At the time, we lacked over-the-horizon technology such as satellites to predict the path of these storms, and there was little time to warn of the advancing storm. On the day the storm hit us, no one was aware of the danger lurking nearby. My father and three older brothers were already in the city at work, school or away at college. Unfortunately, once they learned of the situation they were forced to shelter in place. My nearly six-year-old sister, Helena and I were attending a nearby grammar school and with the first sign of Hurricane Donna's impending visit we were transported to our own homes. This was in spite of the fact that our home was very fragile and in a low-lying flood zone. In hindsight it would have been safer to stay at school. In the early sixties, the father was traditionally the only bread winner. The mother typically fulfilled the role of homemaker.

In advance of the storm, military vehicles from the local Army and Coast Guard bases were patrolling the neighborhood with loudspeakers telling everyone to evacuate. In the days before cell phones and instantaneous communications, my mother refused to leave because she knew my dad would not know where to find us. Besides, she needed to have dinner on the table for Dad when he finally came home.

As the hurricane made landfall, my mom was putting on a brave face and did her best to act calmly. I could see her lips silently moving and I knew she was saying prayers. Before we lost electrical power, she was busy ironing my dad's shirt for the next workday. Another reason she didn't evacuate was that she neither had a car nor a license to drive one. As the house began to flex and shake, she made a lunch of Campbell's tomato soup and grilled cheese. In the absence of my father and three brothers, I stepped up as the new man in the house and naturally put on a calm demeanor to let my mother and sister, Helena, know that all would be well. I too prayed silently, and stood ready to do some heavy lifting if our house came apart. It was my first time to experience a hurricane's category 2 cyclonic winds. The ocean and bay met and submerged the entire community. We had a trap door that opened to a staircase to the basement and we could see the entire area was flooded. My mother could see cans of food, Christmas ornaments and a Nativity Scene floating in the flood waters. After losing power, I was the one who swam through our basement to retrieve these items.

As I handed them up to Helena, her face was streaked with tears and she was completely hysterical. The howling winds and changing conditions had her in a total panic. This was the most devastating experience she'd witnessed in her brief life. She would turn six only nine days later. For the rest of the storm, I stood next to her to keep her calm. As she regained her composure, tear streaks began to evaporate as the storm drifted away. To this day she has vivid memories of the event and she still has the Nativity scene I rescued in my basement swim. Despite my young age, I did my best to assume the role of leadership and demonstrate my courage. By presenting a calm appearance, I helped to create an environment that would help us to survive the fury of the storm. This experience would have a strong impact on me personally and would ironically prepare me for future hurricanes that would become a part of my life.

I studied everything I could about hurricanes. As a pilot I was naturally interested in meteorology. I knew most storms originated off the coast of the Sahara Desert in Africa and moved in random tracks across the Atlantic Ocean. The direction of the tracks was mostly determined by the upper atmosphere. The photos taken from the geo-stationary satellite orbits depicted these storms as giant meandering drunken monsters carrying death and destruction in their path. Sometimes an existing high-pressure system would act as a blocker and force the hurricane's low-pressure system to move in another direction. If the hurricane made landfall and moved inland, it would lose its strength and eventually break up. This would happen because the storm system was no longer gaining its source of energy from the warm surface waters of the ocean. The seasonal warmth of the top surface water provided the fuel to build these storms into huge meteorological engines of destruction containing cyclone-like winds pushing mountains of angry ocean water. With the warmer water in the northern latitudes the storms were able to retain their strength and visit the area more frequently. Recently, a hurricane was able to make it to Ireland. Whether you call it global warming or the Earth's temperature cycle, the water was warmer, causing massive areas of the Arctic to melt. In the summer season the shipping lanes were open, allowing maritime traffic to travel east and west above the North American continent. It was also allowing more hurricanes to frequently travel to northern latitudes and do so later in the hurricane season.

Everyone thought that Superstorm Sandy was a once-in-a-seven-hundred-year storm, though I did not subscribe to that train of thought. A week after Sandy we experienced a Nor'easter which is very close to a hurricane. I actually thought that these hurricanes were a giant temperature exchanger. In September of 1999, Hurricane Dennis made landfall in North Carolina and twelve days later Hurricane Floyd made landfall in the same area. The warm water fueled the storms and in exchange the storms gained more power. If in the wake of Sandy, the water was still warm, we could get another storm and it could happen well after the official end of hurricane season. The sudden visit of yet another hurricane could potentially destroy our neighborhood. The next hurricane could carry greater strength and happen sooner. I would feel more comfortable to hear that the ocean temperatures had cooled and were no longer able to fuel yet another destructive "goliath." This, combined with my aversion to arson, were the greatest fears which I couldn't share. In the case of another hurricane strike it could cause many people to panic. Either way it was best not to speak about them and focus on the positive.

Silently, I prayed neither would happen. I needed to re-establish the firehouse and return the organization to a full operational capability as soon as possible. I also needed to develop a reliable method to report any fires and alert our firefighters. Our Security Patrol employed many retired NYPD cops and they were on a look-out for any arson activity. For several months after Sandy, it felt like my body was in a brace when I awoke. Every muscle in my body was rigid as I relived in my sleep what we had experienced.

Fear is an emotion induced by a perceived danger or threat. The more afraid you feel, the scarier things will seem. There were many other fears that we all experienced. Franklin Delano Roosevelt once said, "The only thing we have to fear is fear itself." Besides the two fears already mentioned, many of us had the fear of the unknown. We were now traveling down a new path that was unknown to all of us.

The Breezy Point community demonstrated their strength and courage during the 9/11 attacks. They lost more than thirty people. Many residents worked at Ground Zero helping to find the remains of fellow first responders. Now many of them were dying of 9/11 re-lated illnesses. How much adversity could one community handle? Just being located on the seashore, the people of Breezy Point were strong from weathering winter storms. During Sandy, one resident who worked in the fishing industry, actually used a Sharpie to write her name and social security number on her forearm to help identify her in case of her demise.

As our recovery progressed, we made many minor triumphs. One of my fears would be regressing to the primitive state we faced af-ter the storm. I didn't want to lose any gains we fought so hard to achieve. One of these areas was the need to have a continuous flow of fuel for our generator, heater and trucks. Sandy wiped out many of the piers in New York Harbor that serviced the fuel barges. As a result, the area suffered a severe fuel shortage. The fuel was a necessity to make the fire house habitable and to respond to emergency calls.

My fear was that the fuel we were getting was so sporadic that it would dry up quickly. Sea Bass, through his contacts at the NYPD, was able to get the PBFD added to the list of Emergency Operations Centers and we received daily fuel deliveries on a steady basis.

Despite this, we knew that the arrangement was fragile and at any minute could be by-passed due to a higher requirement.

My fears also turned to issues related to our health. During the fire when we were overcome by the firestorm and later traversing the smoke plume at least three times, I knew we were exposed to many dangerous particulates. The homes ravished by the fire were built in the 1930s and 1940s with material that would now be considered hazardous. My other worries included the failure of the federal government to help the community in its recovery. The Rockaway Peninsula served as a natural barrier to mainland New York City. Some current schools of thought suggested that seashore communities should be abandoned after a disaster due to their vulnerability to rising sea levels and future storms.

Fraudulent or bankrupt insurance companies were a constant worry. There was a real fear of fraudulent contractors and other scammers. We heard reports of looters making nighttime visits and feared for our safety. Ignorance fueled our fears but information became power and helped quell our emotions. However, we all knew our vulnerability left us susceptible to a whole universe of scammers. We quickly learned to keep our fears in check and share our confidence and cheer with others. Intuitively, we knew the absence of fear in the face of adversity would lead us to success. During World War II the British originated the phrase, "Keep Calm and Carry On." The people of Breezy remembered the term and in a short time, T-Shirts with the slogan were ever present in the community. It has been often said that the eagle has no fear of adversity. The entire community was quickly adapting a fearless spirit.

CHAPTER **10**

Picking up the Pieces

IMMEDIATELY AFTER SANDY, Breezy Point was uninhabitable. Nearly every home was impacted by the flood or fire. None of the essential services such as water, electric or gas were working. Despite its close proximity to New York City, the place looked like a war-torn center. The

entire place was a mess and it was difficult to pick a starting point.

Our early decision to talk to the press and tell them our good news story, was working well and an early decision to turn to the internet and social media was producing results. We needed to accomplish two very important roles: maintain a fire response capability and re-build our firehouse. After a team meeting, we decided to move out of the existing firehouse and set up a provisional firehouse nearby.

Tim Dufficy offered his house on the north side near the bayside. It survived the storm and sustained relatively little damage. It was large enough to house some of the firefighters and had a generator to provide electricity, lighting, and some heat. He had enough space to store our bunker gear and the limited amount of usable equipment that survived the storm. Inside, we set up a table to operate our radios and charge batteries. Our trucks were stored in the open air, in an empty lot near his house. We covered them with some plastic tarps but most of the trucks were subject to the natural elements.

We found an old 8 x 4 sheet of plywood and with red spray paint we scrolled "PBFD-Camp Dufficy." It was difficult keeping the personnel together. Everyone had major work to do on their own homes. In some cases, members were moving to less affected areas in Brooklyn, Queens or on Staten Island for temporary lodging. The primitive living conditions in Breezy Point brought about a diaspora that stripped us of much needed manpower.

Half of the core group entirely lost their homes and needed a place to stay while the rest of the places were in desperate need of repair. Some looked forward to the adventure of living a bare bones existence, but that sense of adventure would wear off eventually. We had about seven firefighters staying at Camp Dufficy though I continued to sleep in my own devastated house for a short time. The moisture from the flood was permeating nearly everything in the house. The moisture was spreading vertically and was wicking up the inside of the walls and spreading to the box spring, mattress and bed sheets of my bed. Eventually, I could no longer stay there. Like my fellow homeless friends scattered about New York City, I sought refuge in my second car which happened to survive the storm.

While still living alone in my home and trying to get some sleep, the whole situation hit me like an emotional ton of bricks, luckily with no witnesses. I broke down and cried like a baby. Some were tears of relief, as I recalled the decisions I made that night that turned out to be right. The others were tears of sorrow at the impossible tasks that faced us in the future. I was grateful that no one was able to witness my emotional breakdown because as a leader and chief, I didn't want anyone to see this perceived weakness. I needed to maintain a mask of someone with strength and self-control. Eventually all of us would experience our own breaking point. One of the men was seen in the early morning walking to the water on the bayside also crying like a baby. It became a rite of

PBFD quarters during recovery

passage as we shed our emotional weaknesses and continued to build our inner strength and progressed on this journey out of devastation.

There were volunteers from outside church groups that were handing out pamphlets which contained messages of hope and some carried the message of suicide prevention. It was obvious that this group knew from previous disaster events that their mission was vital. After fighting one of New York City's largest residential fires, we were displaying a false bravado by thinking we were invincible and that these messages did not apply to us. We were wrong and as a leader I should have given more credence to the subject. Later, I would be surprised when one of our members came   close to killing himself by attempted suicide.

The day after the disaster our first steps were to call a truck maintenance company and get them to perform maintenance to prevent these racehorses from meeting an untimely death. They drained all the reservoirs; engine oil, transmission oil, rear differential and front water pump. We found all of the fluids appearing milky white from corrosive salt water contamination. We replaced all of the fluids. We did our best to find fresh water and wash down our trucks.

Our available firefighters split into two groups: one was a team dedicated to responding to fire calls and the other team's job was to make use of any available daylight and restore the firehouse to a habitable condition. Dufficy's Provisional Firehouse was working but as winter approached, we needed a larger facility. We needed to get our existing firehouse cleaned, repaired, brought up to minimum living standards and ready to live in before the cold weather arrived. It was now November 2nd and already snow squalls began to appear. Privately, I actually welcomed the cold weather because I knew it would cool the ocean waters and deny any potential storms of their fuel.

After the floods finally receded, many residents were now able to return to Breezy to start the salvage and recovery process. In most homes there are family photos either in frames or in albums. Usually, these pictures reflect individuals along with their friends and family as they progress through life. For some it was heartbreaking to discover that all was lost. Homes can be rebuilt and new pictures can be taken but too many people can no longer share the photos of their younger years. These are the pieces that can't ever be picked back up.

Seeing the devastation

CHAPTER 11

Being Swarmed by Angels

OUR COMMUNICATION EFFORTS through the Internet, web site, Facebook page and our frequent contacts with the media were paying off. The core group were quick learners and after observing a couple of interviews they readily stepped up to the task. We were approaching the date of the New York Marathon, where runners from all over the world converged on the city. In preparation for the event, Porta Potties were in position and lined the entire marathon's path. It was a disgrace and a slap in the face to everyone affected by the storm. Portable bathrooms were not available for any of the city's disaster

areas. The South Shore of Staten Island, the western coast of Brooklyn near Red Hook and the entire Rockaway Peninsula were without any permanent or temporary sanitary facilities because the city was using them for the runners. Several nights before the start of the marathon, we had a fire call and the news media covered our response. After the job was completed a TV reporter came over for an interview. After she asked me a few questions she turned to one of the core group and started to interview him. I stood in the background proudly watching how he was handling the questions. Towards the end he turned the interview into a statement of why Mayor Bloomberg should cancel the marathon. Initially, I was shocked but as he continued, he made a cogent case about why it should be cancelled. He explained that none of the disaster areas had any means to handle any sanitary conditions and he told the reporter that all Sani Cans were being used for the Marathon and none for the City's disaster areas. Once again, I was proud of the way he handled the interview and hoped that his voice would make a difference..

Someone must have been listening because the next morning the mayor shocked everyone and announced that the Marathon would be cancelled. It was a bold step and unprecedented. Within two days of the interview all of the affected neighborhoods had Sani-cans. I can't help but think that my firefighter's interview had a bearing on the mayor's decision. Once again, the core group made me very happy. Sadly, the thousands of runners who came to the city to run the race were now sidelined, though many of them volunteered to help the communities impacted by the storm. It was an international effort and they were happy to volunteer in our devastated neighborhoods. They were the first 'angels' to descend upon the storm-ravaged communities.

Throughout history, during any war or crisis, we can see examples of outstanding leadership rise to the top from within the ranks. For me that person was Sebastian Danese, nicknamed 'Sea Bass,' a

NYPD Officer. During this whole experience I witnessed the best of humanity and frequently said, "We were swarmed by angels." If I was surrounded by angels, Sea Bass would be the archangel. He was a longtime member of the PBFD but I rarely saw him participating at our drills and meetings before Sandy. He first appeared at our planning meeting for Hurricane Sandy and he became a regular fixture whom I rapidly learned to rely upon. Along with Dufficy, he stood next to me during the night of the fire and impressed me. He demonstrated superb situational leadership throughout the whole ordeal and was young enough to connect with the core group and able to demonstrate strong leadership. It was obvious that he cared about people and managed to take leave from the NYPD. Later he was detailed by the police commissioner, Ray Kelly, to work full time with us. He was a constant fixture and my go-to guy whenever I needed something important to be done. Out of his own pocket, he would lay out money to buy pizza and our other favorite foods to keep morale up and our guys entertained. He was intelligent, strong and an excellent communicator, and successfully liasoned with the FDNY and NYPD to obtain needed supplies.

In wartime events, when generals would come across people like Sea Bass, they would give them a battlefield commission. Many of the PBFD officers were absorbed with their own personal problems caused by Sandy and were not available. This leadership void needed to be filled. My leadership team consisted mostly of Tim Dufficy and my brother, John. They were a great help but I needed more assistance. Normally when we select officers for leadership positions within the department, it is at our annual business meeting and is voted upon by the membership. I couldn't wait that long. We were operating as a skeleton organization and desperately needed to expand my leadership base. I exercised my authority as chief of the department and commissioned 'Sea Bass' as a captain. He immediately assumed the role and welcomed the assignment. It was a gutsy move on his part to step into a leadership position in the midst of chaos.

Sebastian was without a home and all of his property was destroyed in the flood. He was under stress and not in his best disposition, but he knew that the firefighters he led would be in the same condition. On a good day, leading a volunteer organization is a difficult task. In a disaster scenario, the degree of difficulty became exponential. Any good decision would be easily forgotten and any bad decision would be greatly magnified. His career as a NYPD police officer gave him the thick skin to deflect any annoying criticism. Like the training I received as an Air Force pilot, his law enforcement training taught him to stay calm and think on his feet in any emergency. I knew his selection as captain would bring success. He assumed the role so well, that later some of the firefighters would say Sea Bass thought that he was an appointed assistant chief.

Sea Bass would shudder and resist the mention of him being called any kind of angel and certainly didn't come equipped with wings or robes but his conduct was exemplary. Although some of us were altar boys in the past, being referred to now as a saint or angel could be considered inappropriate. They most likely would lower their heads and say, "I was just doing my job."

The first time I heard that expression, I was a kid watching the TV show "Dragnet." It was the closing remarks from an episode, when the star of the show, Sergeant Joe Friday, was explaining to a grateful person and said, "No need to thank me, ma'am, I was just doing my job." At that time, I never knew that those words would become a mantra for myself and many of my friends.

I spent much of my time shuttling back and forth from the provisional firehouse at Camp Dufficy to our abandoned firehouse which needed a total rebuild. I found an abandoned bicycle that survived the storm and used it to travel the eighth of a mile distance on my multiple daily trips between the two stations. We needed to accomplish a massive clean-up, rebuild the firehouse, and prepare it for our winter quarters. We also needed to be on alert to launch at a second's notice when the call for help came in. I never knew when we would get a call for a major fire so I made sure my bunker gear was always with me.

One day while riding the bike and fully decked out with my chief's helmet and bunker gear I met two neighbors who lived near Camp Dufficy. One neighbor was the son of the ailing senior citizen we rescued when we discovered the fire jumped to this area and the other resident was a very successful businessman and owner of a major supermarket. After some small talk, the owner of the supermarket asked me what he could do to help. I was tempted to give him the standard denial response of, "We're doing fine." His eyes were very serious; and I knew he would only accept an honest answer. I was tempted to low ball any request and say we needed some cases of bottled water and some dry socks but I knew he wouldn't accept that answer as well. I looked at the dilapidated bicycle I was sitting upon and visualized how ridiculous I looked dressed in my bunker gear and fire chief helmet. I hesitantly responded with, "What we really need is a replacement chief's utility vehicle equipped with radios, lights and sirens," and then I added quickly, "The Chief of the Rockaway Point Volunteer Fire Department needs the same thing." I maintained my eye lock with him and held my breath awaiting his response. I figured you can't hit the moon if you aim for the ground. He reached into his pocket for his flip phone and immediately ordered two utility trucks for the Volunteer Fire Departments. I was in shock –amazed that he made such a rapid and generous decision. Both departments had their new vehicles the following morning. We were on our way to restoring ourselves as a department.

We had received a call from a Florida Christian Church and they informed us that they were sending a member of their congregation to our firehouse to help in our recovery. It seemed like he just appeared. He was a tall lanky guy in his mid-thirties and could have passed as a drifter. We didn't know how he got here because he didn't have a car, only a few belongings, and a little money. The only thing different between him and the rest of us was his long-disheveled hair. From the start he impressed me as a gentle, loveable person who also came across sometimes as a "character." If we were making a movie, I would cast him as Chewbacca. By now the core group and I looked like a mess and we were starting to get the vacant thousand-yard stare. The term thousand-yard stare came from the unfocused stare that war weary combat soldiers had on an object very far away. He said he was here to work and I welcomed him with open arms. As I shook his hand, he said his name was "Road Dog." By now, I knew angels came in all shapes and sizes and I hoped that Road Dog was going to be a "good angel." He said he always wanted to be a firefighter. With outside help starting to come in from all quadrants, I was assigning the new volunteers to help the members of the PBFD to get some critical work done on the firehouse and to help some members to get some critical work done on their homes. In theory, if their homes were less of a burden, they could provide greater availability to the firehouse. Road Dog was strong and he enjoyed the "grunt work." Someone donated a utility trailer for our use and we built a small room for him and called it the "Dog House." He placed his few possessions in one corner and found a cot and sleeping bag. I told him we were lucky in that we received some cases of water and we were able to get a Porta-Potty from the Marathon. Quite frequently people would bring some food and leave it in the "Back Room" and on rare occasions an American Red Cross food truck would bring some hot meals. I cautioned him and others that we didn't have any refrigeration and we needed to ensure that the food didn't spoil. I introduced him to our "bare bones existence" and did my best to welcome him to our "Disaster World" that existed within the shadows of one of the world's most thriving cities. I'm sure to the outsider it looked like our lifestyle resembled that of a group of homeless people in a less-than-developing Third World country. Road Dog became an added value and his reputation as a hard worker spread rapidly.

It seemed like he never slept and since we lacked any fire alarm system, I needed him to patrol the area, especially at night. The neighborhood was virtually empty and defenseless. I needed to guarantee that any would-be arsonist would not be trying to burn it down. We found another abandoned and operable bicycle and his assignment was to patrol the area and be on the lookout for any signs of fire.

He was all over the community helping many people–especially the elderly. I met my friend who was the chief of the security department and he asked me about Road Dog. The security chief, a retired NYPD Captain, was a good guy and he shared with me some negative comments from the locals about Road Dog. Despite all of the good works he was doing for the people, many of the locals were concerned about his appearance, specifically his wild hair style. Because of all of the debris removal, none of us looked presentable but it was Road Dog's wild and mangy hair that distinguished him in a negative sense. This reminded me of growing up in the sixties when Hippies and war protestors chose to wear similar hairstyles. Everyone disliked any adult or parent criticizing one for their mangy hairstyle. I didn't want to be that person because I appreciated his valuable contributions to the community.

One of our firefighters, Tiny, was a "Bouncer" in a Manhattan nightclub. Through him, we became friends with the club owner who ran several fundraisers to support the PBFD. I gave the manager a call and discussed some of the complaints regarding Road Dog. He had already met Road Dog and, like us, knew that he was a special person. I suggested to the owner of the club that we have another fund raiser for the PBFD and this time the highlight of the event would be having a professional barber give Road Dog a haircut and shave. The owner liked the suggestion and now my challenge was to sell Road Dog on the idea.

Road Dog and I were going to Rockaway to pick up supplies for the firehouse and I had him alone in my car as a captive audience. I mentally prepared for the conversation and knew that I didn't want to come off as some parent from the late sixties telling him he had to cut his hair. I knew he wanted to someday become a firefighter. In my discussion with him I mentioned that many firefighters liked handlebar mustaches. A wet mustache could cool a face in a bad fire and could also catch their snot as it ran out of their nostrils. Long hair and a beard could be a safety hazard in that they could catch on fire and obstruct a Self-contained Breathing Apparatus (SCBA) mask. I explained to him my idea to have a fund raiser at the night club with him getting a hair-cut and a shave as the main event. He loved the idea and jumped at the opportunity. In a short amount of time flyers for the event were made both electronically and in regular print. The event was a sellout and raised a significant amount of money for the firehouse. It was an all-round win-win situation: Road Dog's ego received a big boost, we raised funds for the fire house and we no longer received complaints from some of our concerned citizens. The only problem we had was that many people could no longer recognize Road Dog. He was a love-able person with a big heart. Several months later, on December 27th, we had a dying whale drift up on our shore. Road Dog was one of the first to get a pressurized hose to spray fresh water on the dying mammal in an effort to save the whale's life.

After several months of continuous volunteering and countless hours of hard labor Road Dog told us that his parents lived in Rochester, New York and he was going to visit them. As he was preparing to leave, I thanked him from the bottom of my heart for all of his contributions. He seemed to disappear as quickly as he appeared. Sometimes when angels descend upon us, they come with reasonable-sounding stories about where they came from and where they are going. He was an amazing person and I'm sad to say I never knew his real name but then again, most angels don't have real names.

The constant stream of visiting angels continued. It was like an army that constantly bombarded us with kindness, generosity and a willing-ness to elevate us from our current misery. My daughter, Erin Adams, was one of those angels. Despite living in Connecticut with her husband and four children, she found the time to travel to Breezy Point on an almost daily basis. Each day she stepped into the firehouse carrying boxes of do-nuts and containers filled with fresh coffee. She was a bright and cheery addition to our dismal landscape. She was ready to lend a hand in our clean-up effort and would walk about the community offering help to strangers who were in dire need. She brought a positive attitude and her smile made everyone momentarily forget their dire circumstances.

She was able to energize the people of her Connecticut neighborhood and get them to adopt our community in this time of need. The people of Wilton and her church conducted a clothing drive and donated much needed supplies. At various stages of the recovery, they collected items necessary at that phase. Initially we needed cases of water, contractor grade trash bags and dry socks. Later we needed brooms, shovels and other assorted tools. Erin discovered a rather large pile of our Class A uniforms, ready to be thrown out in a dumpster. The uniforms were badly soiled and looked like they were unsalvageable. She collected the uniforms and delivered them to the Wilton Dry Cleaners where the owner inspected them and said he could clean them. He insisted on doing it pro bono. It would have cost us a few thousand dollars to replace them. At the time we didn't know it but in our not-too-distant future we would need those uniforms to represent the department at some high visibility events.

In her spare time, she found a charitable organization making very significant donations to several communities affected by Superstorm Sandy. A review of the listed communities receiving donations failed to include Breezy Point. She spent many hours on the phone with the program manager from the charitable organization and successfully convinced this person to add Breezy Point to the list of donation recipients. Many of her neighbors found the time to travel to Breezy and lend their hands and backs to the massive cleanup effort. One neighbor actually loaned the firehouse his gas-powered generator. It was small but able to power a few lights and a radio. The radio provided welcome sounds to our ears and helped to briefly transport us to a better place. This little capability became a huge morale boost in that we were able to do simple things like raising the engine deck doors electronically. Each improvement brought us closer to moving back into the firehouse on a full-time basis. Later we would get an industrial-sized generator that would fully support our essential requirements.

Like the challenges faced by Americans in the Reconstruction Era after the Civil War, Breezy Point and the whole Rockaway Peninsula faced many challenges, and difficult decisions needed to be made. I was in a unique position to witness these events. Besides being the PBFD Chief during Sandy and the recovery, I was an elected member of the Breezy Point Board of Directors and also a member of the Queens County, New York City, Community Board 14.

Each organization had strong leaders in place who eagerly approached the new challenge facing us. The entire eleven-mile Peninsula was in ruins. The residents of the area represented a thorough cross section of the economic spectrum. Superstorm Sandy was an equal opportunity disaster provider and did not discriminate against people no matter their economic or social status. The frequency of organizational meetings quickly doubled and meeting agendas included how to deal with insurance claims, avoid disreputable contractors and most importantly, how to navigate the complicated maze of city, state and federal red tape. The people on the whole peninsula were focused on restoring the area to pre-Sandy levels and many were bold enough to think about bringing the Rockaways to a higher level. For many years, visionary leaders from the eleven seaside neighborhoods saw a "Rockaway Renaissance" in the making. The Rockaways were being re-discovered by developers as a dynamic and trendy area. Many feared that after Sandy struck the area, that the sense of a "renaissance" would evaporate. Instead, the devastation created by Sandy was seen as an opportunity to weed out old dilapidated structures and replace them with modern and safe buildings that added to the aesthetic value of the entire area. Visionary people like State Assemblyman Phil Goldfeder, the community board staff and other community leaders saw Sandy as an opportunity to turn it into an urban renewal project. It was an opportunity, if used properly, that would allow the "Rockaway Renaissance" to accelerate and transform the entire area into a classic district within New York City, attractive to both seasonal tourists and year-round residents.

Besides my daughter, many other family members jumped in to lend their support. Several distant relatives made anonymous and generous donations to the rebuild effort. My brother John knew my living conditions were deplorable. I initially lived in my house where the receding waters left enough moisture to transform it into a giant petri dish of mold and mildew. When it became uninhabitable, I used my car as a place to sleep. John came to my rescue and suggested I stay at his home in Bay Ridge, Brooklyn. After putting in my standard sixteen-hour day, a dry bed, a hot shower and a cooked meal were a welcome sight. My sister-in-law Maureen always managed to keep me in a healthy supply of clean clothing.

John was a sixty-year member of the PBFD and his heart was dedicated to the department. At this time, he served as a New York State Supreme Court judge. He had boundless energy and when we joined up in the evening after our exhaustive days of work, the both of us would pull up the computer and review email messages from other volunteer fire departments around the country and private citizens who were interested in making financial donations. The midnight communications helped to bring the continued stream of angels to our aid. John took over the receipt of all donations and kept a running record of all donations.

Since the PBFD was a certified non-profit organization, anyone making a financial contribution was entitled to a tax deduction as long as they had a document from the non-profit organization to validate the claim. We were happy to accept the donations but with the chaos and devastation, we lacked the administrative staff and equipment to produce these letters to our generous donors. Unless I developed an administrative plan to rectify the situation, I would be facing a new level of chaos as tax time approached. Once again, I found outstanding support from a family member. My brother David's daughter, Cathy Ingram, was a fund raiser for a major college. She was the director of program development and alumni affairs and her job was to help find donors to support the college. She was fully experienced in how to produce correspondence to solicit support and most importantly how to properly document the donations so that donors could receive a tax exemption for their effort.

I still had the fear that we could be attacked by yet another storm before the end of the year. I wanted to rebuild the firehouse so that we had two levels and could house firefighters and survivors on the upper level just in case we were to soon experience yet another hurricane. I also wanted to elevate the engine deck so that in case of another flood the trucks would be above the high-water line. My brother Tom was an architect and an inactive member of the PBFD. I approached him and told him about my concerns for a two-story firehouse. I asked him to re-activate his membership in the PBFD and to start drawing up plans for a new firehouse.

I also didn't want to spend a significant amount of money rehabilitating our existing structure only to knock it down while constructing a new building. The new plans would need to be integrated with the current restoration efforts so that the work projects would not be duplicated. Tom jumped right in and developed some intricate plans that reflected current standards and codes. The only problem was that our membership was mostly absent, and those who were present couldn't agree upon anything. The project sank in the mire of local politics and I knew if we were to be visited by yet another storm, we would have to endure it like we did with Sandy.

Breezy Point is a community of families. Each family was a microcosm of my own and the others reached out to their friends and relatives in a similar fashion. Many people had great childhood memories of the place and although they moved away and hadn't visited in a long-time, they were willing to come to our aid in this time of need. Our army of angels was fully staffed and dedicated to the resurrection of our community. It was a privilege to witness these angels in action and to see the best side of humanity.

Like the floodwaters of Sandy, we were now being inundated with critically needed items. We did not have the resources or the space to manage these donations. It was a problem that we welcomed and we quickly developed a plan to manage the situation. We again commandeered the clubhouse and turned it into a disaster relief distribution center. In a short amount of time, we filled the place with much needed clothing, food and clean-up supplies. We were critically short of staff to run the center and decided to use the honor system and let people have access to the building. We instructed them to take what they most needed and to leave the rest for others. It was a risky plan but once again the people did not disappoint. The distribution center was unlocked and permitted twenty-four-hour access. There were many grateful people seen leaving the place with arms and bags full of highly coveted items.

Sea Bass became friends with a group of people who banded together to help make a difference. Many of them were retired FDNY firefighters and others were friends of FDNY. Sea Bass and I welcomed this group and decided to become their partners. This embryonic group quickly sprouted up and adopted the organizational name "Gut and Pump." We had donations that we wanted to be dispersed to multiple people instead of just one. The Gut and Pump group set up a system where tools were loaned out with specific instructions on when to return them. It was like a library book lending system. This allowed for multiple users and prevented hoarders from absconding with the critically-needed tools for limited use. Someone donated to the PBFD a

Gut and Pump Volunteers

large army tent with several rooms. We assigned the tent to the Gut and Pump organization and they used it as their headquarters to store and distribute equipment in the large parking lot adjacent to the clubhouse. Before long they acquired a generator that ran the lights, computers, heater and other office equipment. When the weather was warm, they slept there and when the winter arrived, they moved in with us after we re-claimed the firehouse. They were great people dedicated to their noble purpose.

Erin Corcoran, a former New York State Court Officer and a former member of the Rockaway Point Fire Department, assumed a key leadership position within Gut and Pump. She was currently employed as an assistant prosecutor in Florida and was working with us on a leave of absence. She did an outstanding job and we made her an honorary firefighter of the PBFD. At night they usually set up a small fire pit and sang songs and told stories about the events they were experiencing. From a distance I'm sure they all looked like a camp of homeless people. Like Road Dog, it seemed as if they never slept. It is said that angels also never sleep. They are too busy doing their important work. Our nest of angels made a valuable contribution and several months later they were invited to the White House to be honored for their actions.

Before Sandy the people of Breezy Point were always digging deep into their own pockets to help others in need. They were always on the giving end but after Sandy they were on the receiving end. Many people felt uncomfortable and embarrassed to be in this situation, but out of necessity adapted to the new situation. After Hurricane Katrina, a Category 3 hurricane, hit New Orleans a group of New York City Firefighters and Police officers banded together to bring supplies and manpower to the area. They knew that the New Orleans police officers and firefighters would be working 16-18 hours a day to restore a semblance of order to their devastated city. The NYPD and the FDNY First Responders also knew that none of their counterparts in New Orleans would have any energy left to try to fix their own homes. They made many lifetime friendships and when Hurricane Sandy hit New York City they knew they had to return the favor.

The police ten codes were developed to cut down the verbiage on police radio calls. In New Orleans the code for assistance to an officer is 1055. Jeff Winn, a New Orleans police officer, organized a group of a dozen first responders from New Orleans and aptly named the group, "NYC 1055." Either through the PBFD's electronic request for help over social media or because they knew that Breezy Point was a community of retired and active cops and firefighters, they chose the PBFD to be their base of operations. They spent a couple of weeks raising funds and gathering equipment and food for the trip. They knew they had a short window in which to visit. They left New Orleans after Thanksgiving and wanted to leave New York City before the first snowfall. They didn't know how they would adapt to the colder temperatures and they knew that no one on their team knew how to drive in the snow.

The caravan consisted of a Winnebago camper and several vans. They knew they had to be self-sufficient and they didn't want to be a burden upon anyone. Jeff Winn said their journey was a no brainer. They all knew what was going through our minds and perhaps more importantly they knew what lay ahead for us all. As first responders and former service members we were taught how to stay cool when under pressure but we were never trained on how to act after the pressure was removed. Instead of decompressing we were mentally beating ourselves up for a variety of reasons. Ironically, for many of us this would be the worst period of time. Our new friends from New Orleans knew this because they had the misfortune to travel down this road before us.

Jeff said that upon their arrival it was surreal. "It was a hell of a sense of 'déjà vu.' he said. "The sheer magnitude of destruction from the hurricane and fire is overwhelming and seemed greater than Hurricane Katrina."

While they were adjusting to our colder temperatures we were adjusting to their accents. At one point the word got out that they had great tasting food. They had lines of people from a variety of volunteer groups like America Corps waiting for food. Once they realized they were nearly out of supplies they called back to one of their donors who owned a New Orleans restaurant. He in turn activated his network of friends who were restaurant owners in New Jersey and New York and managed to get a continuous replenishment of their supplies. Their hospitality, great food and friendship at a critical time helped us immensely and made for lifetime friendships. They helped to restore over thirty homes of cops and firefighters from Breezy Point who were still working endlessly to resurrect New York City.

From my experience as a disaster response officer, I learned that many states developed "Mutual Aid Agreements" (MAA) with other state partners. In these agreements it was understood that many local first responders would be absorbed with their own personal problems and unable to perform their own duties. The MAAs were usually made with a state geographically removed from the state affected by the disaster. They in turn would provide personnel to backfill the vacancies created by personnel who couldn't report to duty.

The NYC 1055 Group also used the name "NOLA Til Ya Die." It was the mantra and "war cry" used by the people in New Orleans during their recovery. Jeff Winn taught us that we had to create an avenue or forum in which to decompress. As leaders during a disaster, we didn't have the luxury to dwell on a decision. After the external pressure was lifted, it was then that we realized the decisions we made could have had dire consequences. Often, we sent people into dangerous positions from which their return was doubtful. In the aftermath we realized how close we came to having a negative outcome. Both Jeff Winn and I knew that we lived through separate but similar experiences, and that we would be forever changed. It was very likely that we would never achieve full normalcy after the experience. In the same breath, we agreed that it was an experience we will never forget. Later we would be visited by another famous person from New Orleans. Harry Connick, Jr. came and put on an impromptu concert that raised our spirits. The angels appeared from everywhere. Even my financial advisor, Mike McMurray, filled up his Winnebago with supplies and dropped them off at the PBFD.

I retired from my 41-year civil service career as a senior manager with the FAA's Flight Standards Division in August 2012 right before

Superstorm Sandy changed all of our lives. As part of my retirement celebration, Nancy and I booked a cruise for November 2012. We did this long before we ever heard of Sandy. I knew if I cancelled the cruise, I would lose a lot of money. Besides, with all of the stress during and after Sandy, I really needed the break. In preparation for my week-long absence, I appointed Sea Bass as the "acting chief." Since assuming the role of captain, he demonstrated he was very capable in both the firefighting side and the people side of the department. He continued to build a great relationship with Gut and Pump and NOLA. He forged a great relationship with the NYPD and was able to get their outstanding support. Our good friend, Gary Urbanowitz, also helped us in this area. He was another angel who landed on our engine deck. Gary is an Honorary FDNY Deputy Chief, FDNY historian and author and later became the executive director of the New York City Fire Museum. During his visit he became close with the core group and provided moral support for them during this stressful time. He helped rebuild several homes of our firefighters. He also assisted Sea Bass in building a database designed to provide information to the people of Breezy regarding resources to assist in rebuilding their homes and the community. His efforts were significant and contributed greatly to the ongoing history of the PBFD.

On his own, Sea Bass gracefully handled the numerous phone calls from potential donors. One phone call was from a California real estate developer who wanted to bring a dozen volunteers and Sandy survivors to a new desert community to wine and dine them with hopes of getting some publicity for the developer. He handled the request and many others in an outstanding fashion. In a short amount of time, he learned to juggle many glass balls without dropping one. When I returned, the place was upright and running like a top. I quickly discovered that in a spirit of goodwill he handed out our entire supply of PBFD tee shirts and hats. He also made two people honorary firefighters. Normally the selection of an honorary member was reserved for the elected chief in concurrence with the board of commissioners. We couldn't undo the situation if we wanted to, but I was lucky that the two people he appointed were highly deserving. I was able to calm down some ruffled feathers and graciously congratulate the new honorary members.

My biggest concern upon returning from my retirement cruise was the core group. My quick vacation cruise allowed me to view our firehouse situation as if I were an outsider. The most obvious concern was the appearance of each member of the core group. For over a month they were constantly ensconced in their new disaster world. They were working long days with little food and poor sleeping conditions. Their "thousand-yard stare" was more pronounced. It was shouting at me and I knew they needed a break. The family of one of our members owned a large ski house in the Catskills. We developed a plan so that they could get a total break from their disaster world and visit the ski house for some much-needed rest and relaxation. Many of the core group initially refused to go and felt that they were being disloyal to the department and the community. After some quiet conversation that also included some of my classic animal metaphors, they finally agreed to leave for a short break. Sometimes when you are involved in a marathon effort like a recovery from Superstorm Sandy, you need to take the time to recharge the batteries.

We continued to have many people call us with plans to volunteer with some of the cleanup efforts for the firehouse and for the homes of some of our members. One of the major problems was, as the community cleaned out the debris from their homes, they piled it up in the sand lanes near their homes. This created a logjam and prevented emergency vehicles access to the area. Many of our volunteers helped us to clear the sand lanes and bring the debris to a central location where the New York City Sanitation trucks could cart it away. Eventually, there were mountains of refuse that contained old appliances, wood decking, furniture, couches, pianos and everything you would find in a home. At night the NYC Sanitation Department would carry it to a very large parking area in nearby Riis Park. It was then sorted and separated for recycling and shipped to a variety of areas for processing.

The phone calls from the volunteers absorbed a considerable amount of time. After I spent a lengthy time on the phone giving them directions, many of them failed to show up. Breezy Point is made up of the three separate communities of Roxbury, Rockaway Point and Breezy Point. Each community has their own volunteer fire department. I eventually figured out that the volunteers were indeed coming but stopping at the first volunteer house they saw. Initially, I was upset that all of the work speaking to these prospective volunteers was for nothing. I quickly realized that it was equally important that each community utilized the volunteers. It didn't make sense to have one community segment be a "Tidy Bowl" while the others were still struggling. In the aviation safety business, we said the aircraft didn't crash by compartments, but rather when it crashed it was the whole aircraft. In a similar sense the Breezy Point community would not survive unless all three individual communities recovered.

In early December we closed up shop at Camp Dufficy and returned to the firehouse. The place was clean and habitable, but was also a work in progress. Some of our best help came from the United States Marine Corps. They were part of the federal disaster response force. In typical Marine fashion they made an amphibious landing and established a beachhead on our shoreline complete with a helicopter landing zone. They set up tents with communications and a "chow hall." Earlier they made

Marines and sailors assigned to the 26th Marine Expeditionary Unit step off a landing craft utility vehicle onto the shore of Breezy Point, a small coastal community in New York, No. 8, 2012. They and troops from other units are partnering with the Federal Emergency Management Agency, the U.S Army Corps of Engineers and the National Guard to help the residents of New York City return to normalcy as soon as possible. U.S. Marine Corps photo.

a similar amphibious landing on the shores of Staten Island but failed to give local authorities advance notice. It caused a big brouhaha with many residents thinking they were being invaded. We quickly became good friends with the Marines and their assistance helped us to accelerate our return to the firehouse. We were honored when they asked us to host their 237th birthday celebration on November 10th at our firehouse. My brother John, a retired rear admiral, in the New York Naval Militia was one of the speakers at the birthday celebration.

Each year the PBFD conducted a Christmas party for the neighborhood kids. It was a holiday classic and it attracted many former members and their kids. Although many people were not back in their homes, we felt that it would be a first step to bring back a sense of normalcy to our routine. We also knew the kids were deeply impacted by the destruction of Sandy. Before Sandy, we had a stockpile of gifts for the kids but that was all destroyed in the hurricane. Part of the tradition was to have Santa Claus arrive at the firehouse on a firetruck and later take the kids for a ride on the rig with lights and sirens signaling their passage. Besides not having any gifts for the kids, we were reluctant to use our trucks for other than essential usage. Our problems would once again be solved by some visiting angels.

Cliff Falman was a former volunteer firefighter from Westchester County, New York and a full-time chiropractor now practicing in Aruba. Because of his status as a chiropractor and his past experience, he had key contacts within the Aruban Fire Department and key government officials. Cliff had learned about us through social media and knew about our plan of having a 'Kids Christmas Party" within a disaster-ridden community. He banded together with his friends in the Aruban Fire Department and they used their collective influence to approach the Aruban Bureau of Tourism with a plan to raise $15,000 worth of gifts for our kids and deliver them to Breezy Point. They also approached JetBlue to voluntarily fly these gifts to JFK International Airport in New York in time for our Christmas party. We first met Cliff at JFK International Airport. He flew on the airplane carrying the gifts and helped us load them onto a firetruck for the short trip to Breezy Point.

Aruba is also known as "One Happy Island" and through their generosity, they made approximately two hundred kids very happy. Any extra gifts were given to the other fire departments. Several times I had to pinch myself to make sure I wasn't just dreaming this--and to realize that Cliff grew up celebrating Hanukah and not Christmas! It was obvious that angels came from all religions, cultures and nationalities and they flew on commercial airplanes!

The "Friends of Rigby Foundation" was founded in 2006 after Dan Rigby died in an off- campus house fire in his senior year of college. Their mission was to improve the safety of off- campus housing and to prevent others from experiencing the same fate as Dan. They discovered us through the social media. We shared areas of overlapping interest with our primary interest in protecting people's lives from fire. They normally made donations to programs that provided safety to students living in off-campus housing. They were having a fund-raising event in a Manhattan theatre and invited us to attend and speak at the event. Dan's brother Patrick was the organizer of the event and when we came together, I felt a close and almost spiritual connection to his deceased brother, Dan. The event was a huge success and they made a generous donation to the PBFD.

Another organization called Direct Relief from Santa Barbara, California, also made a very generous donation to the PBFD. They manufactured fire rescue equipment and coordinated with ABC's Good Morning America, surprising us on live TV to film the presentation of the check.

Through my experience as an Air Force Liaison Officer with FEMA, I learned that common to most disaster responses, people experienced injuries to their feet. Most disaster areas included flooded areas and nearly everyone became susceptible to foot injuries. It is common for people to experience trench foot or immersion foot when the feet are constantly exposed to moisture. With debris scattered all about it is easy for someone to step on an exposed nail. FEMA understands the problem and routinely stocks warehouses around the country with dry footwear and other foot gear to minimize the impact. After several months of exposure to the disaster environment I was in need of medical attention for my feet. I called my friend and Podiatrist Dr. Steve Epstein who had a storefront office in Rockaway Park near the seawall on Jamaica Bay. I hadn't talked to him since before Sandy visited the neighborhood. His entire practice was destroyed during the storm. He still had a medical bag and agreed to make a house call to help me out. When he came to my house it was evident that the Superstorm had a devastating effect upon him. In a short time, he patched me up and he explained that he was moving his practice to the mainland. The trauma of Sandy was too much and he was leaving the area to start all over. He made many other house calls to people on the peninsula who were in need of his assistance.

We were invited to attend the 12-12-12 Concert at Madison Square Garden. It was called the 12-12-12 Concert because it was held on December 12, 2012. The concert was organized by the Robin Hood Foundation and it was officially titled "The Concert for Sandy Relief" and included a list of famous British Rock and Roll stars like Paul McCartney, Eric Clapton, the Who and the Rolling Stones. A list of famous groups from America included local musicians like; Jon Bon Jovi, Kanye West, Bruce Springsteen and Billy Joel. Alicia Keyes was the only solo female performer and she stole our hearts when she sang, "An Empire State of Mind." The concert would go down as one of the

Thanks to Robin Hood Foundation for inviting us to 12-12-12 concert

top twenty events in the history of Madison Square Garden. We were lucky to receive fifteen tickets but it created a big problem since everyone wanted to attend. The people running the concert made a special request and asked us to wear our dress uniforms. Once again, I was glad that the Wilton Dry Cleaners had come to our rescue and rehabilitated our uniforms. Because of the request to wear our uniforms, I sensed that our group might be used for some high visibility segment during the concert. I had no idea how correct my intuition would be.

Having only fifteen tickets made it difficult to select who would attend. We narrowed the selection to the core group and we still had enough staff to provide coverage at the fire house. A trailer carrying multiple showers was recently delivered to the area and helped us to shed our dusty and dirty appearance. Initially it was difficult getting everyone cleaned, showered and dressed. At times I felt like I was herding a group of cats wanting to go in all directions. Within a couple of hours, we changed from a group of rag-tag disaster survivors to a very sharp group that would make any firefighter proud. Our group jumped into the new chief's vehicle and a van from the Firefighter Family Transport organization and traveled north on Flatbush Avenue through Brooklyn, over the Brooklyn Bridge and direct to Madison Square Garden. Our lights and sirens helped us to get through the metallic sludge of New York City traffic in record time.

The Garden was at its maximum concert capacity of 20,000 people and was wired for global television distribution. It was a highly charged festive atmosphere. The PBFD were the only people in uniform and we were easy to spot in a crowd. Each disaster neighborhood impacted by Sandy sat in sections close to the stage. Many of the people I recognized from a variety of TV news and newspaper stories. Many of them had lost relatives during the disaster. There was a woman sitting directly behind me who was from Staten Island and I knew that she lost her husband during Sandy. At one point we made eye contact and without saying a word I nodded in her direction as if to say I recognized her and was sorry for her plight. I gave her a quiet smile and she returned it. For many, it was probably the first time they smiled since Sandy interrupted their lives. I looked over the sections and knew that we were all the walking wounded. The Concert for Sandy Relief was not only raising money for the recovery but for four short hours it was raising our spirits and helping us to forget the dismal settings we would have to return to.

Our group was lined up in a row and I began to notice that they were making frequent visits to the concession area. They explained that they were going for some of the big salted pretzels sold in the concession area. It didn't take me long to figure out that many people easily recognized them in their uniforms and knew they were the firefighters who fought the Big Fire inside of Hurricane Sandy. Their money was no good and everyone was buying them beers as a way of saying thanks for a job well done. I still had the suspicion that we were going to be asked to participate in some highly visible fashion. I gently reminded them that we represented all firefighters by wearing the uniform and I didn't want anyone to embarrass us. In lightning speed, the beer cups disappeared and the entire group was munching on big classic New York pretzels. In between the breaks when the bands and performers were changing out their equipment, the cameras zoomed into the areas where the survivors were seated by their neighborhoods. When it came to our turn American film maker Quentin Tarantino introduced us. As we all stood and waved our arms as if we were some winning Olympic Team the whole place let loose with a roar of applause and multiple television cameras zoomed in on us to capture the moment.

After the Forrest Gump movie, I began to classify major events in my life as "Gump Events." This night was quickly becoming a "Mega Gump Event" and it was not over yet. After the introduction by Quentin Tarantino, the men thought that they were finished with our visibility events and they started to go off to the concession area. I quickly stopped them in their tracks and shared with them that I sensed that we were going to be called upon again. They were disappointed when I said the "no alcohol rule" was still in effect. Naturally they were not happy, but they understood. Shortly after that I was approached by an advance man for the concert management and asked if we could go on the main stage with Paul McCartney as he was finishing the last performance of the concert. I was shocked and had to ask him to repeat his request. After repeating his original request, I let him know we were honored and that we would not disappoint. I was a Beatles fan ever since I was a freshman in Nazareth High School. I was privileged to lead these men into a six-alarm fire inside a hurricane and now I would be leading them through a cheering sea of humanity to be on stage with a famous musician who dated back to my teenage years. Besides being live in front of an audience of twenty thousand people, the television signals were being transmitted globally.

Before I left the firehouse, I picked up a couple of "PBFD Challenge Coins" that we gave to a very select few. I anticipated that at some point I would meet some people worthy of the coin. Before the advance man left, I pulled out one of the two coins and asked him if it would be Ok to give this to Sir Paul. I had never been on a stage like this and the last thing I wanted was to be tackled by security guards as I approached Paul and presented him with the coin. The advance guy took the coin and later came back to say I had a green light to give Paul the coin. I was glad I brought two coins since he never gave me back the other.

We were led through the electrified crowd and brought on stage right behind the curtain. Tim Dufficy and I had the remaining coin and we were discussing taking it out of its plastic case. It was difficult to hear each other with the cheering crowd and the blasting music. A gentleman who must have been part of Paul McCartney's team was curious about what we were holding. I politely explained that I planned to give him the firehouse coin as a token of our appreciation for his performance. The man smiled and said he would greatly appreciate it. He said, "Did you know his father was a firefighter in Liverpool?" I said I didn't know that and indicated I might use that piece of info when I met Sir Paul.

Paul was only about ten feet away and we were separated only by a curtain. As Paul was belting out his last song a massive fireworks display was started. Suddenly, it sounded as if all mayhem was breaking out. Something went wrong with the display and it sounded like Sir Paul was accidently hit by the fireworks. We heard Paul shout, "Stop it! Stop it!" The bright lights were flashing and Dufficy and I looked at each other as we began to assess the situation. I said to Dufficy, "Let's look around for some fire extinguishers and be prepared to knock down any fire. Let's also prepare for some injuries and get the core group ready to jump into action." I couldn't believe this was happening. One minute we were preparing to go live onstage and meet a world-famous rock star, and in another moment, we were preparing to fight a fire and rescue the rock star on a world stage. We were careful not to jump into action too early and possibly embarrass ourselves and tensely waited to see if the situation would resolve itself.

After some very long seconds the stage hands successfully restored order to chaos and the show went on. We were given the signal to move to the front of the stage. I was leading our group and could see Paul up ahead facing the audience next to a podium. His head was down and he must have been reviewing some notes. This looked like the best moment to approach him. I knew if I waited, I would not have another opportunity and the moment would be eternally lost. I walked up to him and using my command voice, "Sir Paul, your father will like this." I must have surprised him because he did a neck snap and turned directly to face me. Several other members of the PBFD gathered around. I reached into my pocket for the coin. As I was presenting it to him, I said, "We are presenting you this firehouse coin on behalf of all of the survivors of Hurricane Sandy. We want to thank you and all of the other performers for the great work you did tonight to support us."

He looked me square in the eye and with a genuine expression of gratitude he expressed his thanks. By now we were swamped by others and the stage was exceeding its capacity. I stepped aside to let others get a chance to be close to Paul. The Chief of the Seaside Heights, New Jersey Police Department came up and presented Paul with a baseball cap bearing their name. Paul put it on and joined the crowd in their festivities. On my "Gump Scale" of lifetime events, this was one of the best and I gave it a "Mega Gump" rating.

At the end we were ushered off the stage to a wide corridor. We passed a photo station where a photographer set up an area to take professional grade pictures for attendees of the event. He approached me to get some shots of the PBFD members in uniform. As he asked me if he could get some photos, I happened to look over my shoulder and saw Sir Paul right behind us surrounded by a huge crowd. I turned to him and asked him to join us and he readily agreed. While the camera man was setting up his equipment, I struck up a conversation with Sir Paul. Since I gave him our coin in front of a worldwide audience, I felt that we were on a familiar friend status and figured I could drop the "Sir" prefix. I put my arm around him and said, "Paul, it is cool that your father was a firefighter."

He responded and said, "Yeah, my mother was a nurse."

I told him, "That's very cool; my wife was also a nurse," With that the photographer took the photo with a blinding flash and Paul and I went our separate ways. Our long-lasting friendship was over, but I knew I was touched by an angel.

The constant stream of angels never ended. Volunteer fire departments from all over the country were donating surplus materials. We were slowly getting back to our full operational capability. Many departments donated older trucks that were deemed excess. We were fearful that after our trucks were under five feet of water that they would fail at any moment. We accepted the truck donations, but knew that it would be a tempo-

Thanking Paul McCartney on stage at Madison Square Garden

rary situation. The problem with the trucks was complex. They did not have four-wheel drive allowing us to drive through the sand lanes and the threading on the hoses, pumps and nozzles did not conform to New York City thread standards. We agreed to take the trucks with the caveat that we may re-gift or sell them to raise money for the recovery. It was important that we had a back-up plan in case either or both trucks suddenly were incapacitated. When most of the disaster results had dissipated, former Chief Kurt Bruder had the responsibility to find other organizations or buyers to use these surplus vehicles. From a distance it looked like we were operating a used car lot for fire trucks. At one point we had a half a dozen trucks for sale.

In my last six years in the USAF, I left the air rescue business and worked in the disaster response business. I was assigned as a liaison officer to the Federal Emergency Management Agency (FEMA) and the First Army.

I learned the entire network of disaster response from the local, state and federal levels and I covered all domestic disasters in the United States east of the Mississippi River. I was fully versed in the mission of Military Support to Civilian Authorities (MSCA). I was asked to make a presentation to FEMA's Training Academy on our disaster response to Hurricane Floyd. This was videotaped and used at the FEMA Academy for training new recruits. After retiring from the USAF, I volunteered for the New York Guard, which was a state defense force. I eventually became the Commanding Officer of the 88th Brigade. This organization was based in New York City and its members were a diverse group of both former active-duty military and those with no prior service experience. The lineage of the 88th Brigade dates back to the Civil War when it was part of the Irish Brigade. The unit had several missions and MSCA was their primary mission. We spent many hours learning how to support the local communities after they experienced a disaster. When Sandy struck, I was the vice commander of the brigade. I had to ask for a leave of absence due to my circumstances. The 88th Brigade was activated and I was proud of these troops when they filtered through the neighborhood offering their help. It was interesting to be part of their leadership team and to be standing on the sidelines as a recipient of their services and expertise. I also saw the FEMA representatives in action. They held their daily briefings and focused upon high priority areas that needed immediate attention. They helped us and the other affected neighborhoods to get critical resources in a timely manner. Toward the end when we were gaining our strength, they quietly reduced their presence and then totally disappeared as we were returning to normal. They worked as angels and fulfilled their roles in a noble and unassuming fashion.

CHAPTER 12

It Don't Come Easy

RINGO STARR'S HIT single, "It Don't Come Easy" is about his love of a girl and how difficult it is to make it happen. His words could also apply to our post-disaster situation where many things aren't easy. The high stress of the disaster and the recovery had a significant impact upon many, especially among the senior citizens of our community. The prospect of having to totally rebuild their lives during this late stage of their lives was too overwhelming. We were proud to say that within Breezy Point no one died during Sandy, but the sad truth was that many people died during the aftermath of Sandy. The "post Sandy era" saw a constant stream of funeral

motorcades and Requiem Masses. Both the clergy and the funeral directors were working overtime. There were multiple causes of death, but most people attributed stress as the underlying cause.

Government politics, red tape, frustrations with the system and sometimes simple petty jealousy were some of the cause factors of this stress. Much of the stress was unnecessary and at times annoying. Residents of the neighborhood went from a pre-Sandy existence which was rather mundane to a post-Sandy existence of having to decide upon how to rebuild, what type of construction, whom to select as a contractor, meeting dishonest contractors, new furniture selection and paint color for interior and exterior surfaces. Filing insurance claims, scheduling contractor availability, overseeing the construction and deciding on major areas such as elevating the home all added to the difficulty everyone experienced. They also had to find the right stores from which to purchase this material during a time when fuel was being rationed. In essence nothing was simple and everything appeared to be an insurmountable problem.

Clear communication was essential during this time. Our cooperative management started a "daily alert" system that was a mass telephone call to residents that focused on critical recovery information. Like the movie Good Morning, Vietnam with Robin Williams starting his war zone commentary with, "Good Morning, Vietnam," Denise Nieble, assistant manager of the Breezy Point Cooperative started her broadcast with the announcement of "Good Morning, Breezy Point." The parallel was obvious and it was a subtle hint that our neighborhood had transformed into a war zone. The information shared was vital and helped many to make important decisions on their road to recovery. A resident, who was a former Air Force Officer and a dentist, started up a Facebook page called "Back to Breezy" which was designed to help those who were on their journey back to their homes in Breezy Point. It became a communication platform where people shared their ideas and problems. He also developed a resource list. It contained a list of contractors and stores recommended for use and also advice on how to navigate the morass of government red tape.

Early in 2013, a town hall meeting was held for those people who lost their homes to fire. Initially the area was called the "fire zone" and later after the entire area was rebuilt it was called "Breezy Heights." The new name was due to conformity with new elevation requirements above flood areas. Their problems were unique and it was their first opportunity to get together. The meeting was held in the clubhouse and the remnants of Sandy's visit were still evident to anyone who spent that horrific night inside the building. I was asked to address the group and give them our perspective of the fire. After a forty-five-minute briefing that included questions and answers, and the details of the fire, I was greatly surprised and relieved when the group gave me and the entire PBFD a standing ovation. Tears came to my eyes and they all knew we were grateful for their support. Later these same people banded together and filed a lawsuit against the Long Island Power Authority (LIPA) for failing to shut off the utilities to the area. LIPA did shut off the utilities on Fire Island but failed to do so on the Rockaway Peninsula. Fire Island did not experience any fires. The Rockaway peninsula had three major fires with Breezy Point being the largest. As of 2022, the litigation has been ongoing for more than eight years.

The Federal Stafford Disaster Assistance and Relief Act is responsible for supporting people impacted by disasters, especially hurricanes. President Obama actually made the declaration for New York State on October 28, 2012 in advance of Sandy's arrival. The only problem was that the purse strings were controlled by Congress. Only limited actions would be accomplished until the House of Representatives signed a spending bill aimed at providing relief for the victims of Sandy. Apparently, the politics within the Republican Party was causing the delay. House Speaker John Boehner and Republican House Majority Leader Eric Cantor were at odds because the majority leader failed to support the speaker during a previous critical fiscal vote. It was now payback time. The bill languished for sixty days post-Sandy and the sixty billion Hurricane Sandy Aid Bill was floundering. It was an example of nasty politics at its best and thousands of Sandy survivors were caught in between. Sandy was the second costliest hurricane in United States history only later to be surpassed by Hurricanes Harvey and Maria in 2017.

At the same time, I was scheduled for an interview with a reporter from the New York Daily News. The interview was supposed to be about the status of our firehouse recovery, but I would quickly see that we were being drawn into the political conflict about signing the Sandy Aid Bill. Fortunately, as a senior manager in the FAA, I received training on how to deal with the press. I knew my responses were walking a delicate line, but I held back from stating any negative political comments. The story covered five pages and included photos of my home stripped down to studs and floor joists and a photo of our less than standard living conditions in the back room of the PBFD firehouse. The story was published on January 3, 2013 and Congress signed the bill on January 6, 2013. I often think that this article had some influence upon Congress to do the right thing.

During this time, I was interviewed by N.R. Kleinfield from the New York Times. I was very impressed by his professionalism and attention to detail. He apparently spoke to many people from within the community and he wrote one of the most detailed, articulate and accurate articles on Superstorm Sandy. Mr. Kleinfeld would make the profession proud.

I spent well over ten hours with him over the phone, giving him our story and helping him to validate or debunk other beliefs. We spent many hours creating a timeline of the events as they happened that night. Maybe it was the "fog of war" but I realized that some of my recollections were not as accurate as I thought.

Many of his questions about the fire were focused on the PBFD's work inside the fire and how we were able to throw water on the fire. I gave him a detailed description of how we were the only fire department to get to the southwest corner and how we initially hooked up to a hydrant on the south side of Gotham Walk and initially experienced good water pressure. This helped us to knock down a major portion of the fire in our area and most importantly stopped the westward advancement of the fire. After approximately an hour, we experienced low water pressure at the nozzle. Dufficy stretched another line to the hydrant on the south side of Ocean Avenue to feed our truck's pump. We then had two hydrants feeding our truck. When our second truck arrived on-scene they hooked up to a hydrant west of our location and pumped water to our lead truck to boost the pressure for the line going to the fire.

Later we learned that 135 homes would be destroyed in the fire. Each was connected to the same water system and as each home collapsed the house water lines ruptured and spewed water all over. This was the cause of our low water pressure problem. There were times, when we were in a "cave of fire," I had to repeatedly order the nozzle man to shut off the nozzle with hopes of rebuilding the pressure. It was a dangerous maneuver, but we really didn't have any other options. We had to do this on multiple occasions. We utilized the time to pull down the vertical remnants of the structures to prevent the embers from going airborne and possibly allowing the fire to jump to a new location.

His article was on the front page of the New York Times on December 24, 2012. I called him after the article was published to compliment him on his work. It was at this point that he cautioned me to not be too trusting of everyone. He wouldn't reveal his source, but he revealed to me that someone was going around saying that the PBFD did not put any water on the fire. Initially I was shocked, but attributed the comments to petty jealousy and the stress of the situation that we all were experiencing. I really did not want to know the source. I reminded the reporter of my explanation of the problems we had, but I assured him that we did place water on the fire. I clearly remembered telling him that at one point I was standing on a wooden deck with flames coming from below and I had to urinate badly. I revealed to him that I actually pissed on the fire. I was glad I didn't make that revelation before he published his article. My explanations of how we put water on the fire, most likely caused him not to touch the whole issue and exclude it from his article.

The problem of adequate hydrant pressure was on-going. Breezy Point's hydrant system is color-coded yellow. It is connected to the same water lines supplying the residential and commercial areas. Activating multiple hydrants from the same water source is like placing multiple straws in a glass of water. When that water supply empties, it doesn't matter how many straws you have in the glass; you will be out of water. It is basically a singular main line whereas in major parts of New York City another main line may be as close as across the street. On the night of Sandy's assault on Breezy Point, when the water line collapsed after the 135 homes were compromised, the entire yellow hydrant system was impacted. The FDNY has a dedicated hydrant line along the main road identified by black hydrants. When FDNY arrived, they tapped into this hydrant system and were successful in getting water to the fire. They needed a significant amount of manpower and resources to run the hoses from this centrally located system to the fire zone.

When we fought our first fire on the northwest side of the property, we tapped into the black hydrant system and had an adequate pressure. We were fortunate in that this water was close to the fire's location. The fire zone was a considerable distance from the black hydrant system operated by the FDNY. Drafting is another system of getting water to a fire. It is mostly used in rural areas and we didn't have the resources to connect our equipment. In the past, we found that the filters could not stop the ever-present shell fragments and they eventually ruined the pump.

In the aftermath of Sandy, the funds appropriated by Congress were divided by each state. In New York State the Governor's Office of Storm Recovery (GOSR) established the NY Rising Community Reconstruction Program (NYRCR) to allocate these funds to areas impacted by Hurricane Sandy. It was a participatory initiative and each community identified projects and implemented actions to become more resilient in the future. Many projects were identified and had to compete against each other for selection. Sadly, the project for an improved hydrant system was not selected.

The visibility we received from the Daily News and New York Times articles was not all necessarily good. I made a commitment to pay serious attention to any prospective person or organization who offered us help. This goes along with the notion that "beggars can't be choosers." I would find out that not everyone was genuine and some bordered upon the lunatic fringe. After the publication of these two articles, I was going about my business in the back room of the firehouse when I received a call from a gentleman who was from New Zealand and currently was visiting in midtown Manhattan. I was fortunate that several of our members and volunteers from "Gut and Pump" were present and overheard half of the conversation.

Behind his Kiwi accent, the man almost sounded desperate, "I need to with speak you in person. I need to explain my plan to help reduce the impact of all disasters on a world-wide basis. It is urgent that I meet with you today."

Worried that this could be a legitimate call and not wanting to miss an opportunity that would extricate all of us out of this disaster, I politely told him, "I'm busy and plan to drive shortly to southern Connecticut to visit some people."

He was still determined and said, "I can meet you at a nearby subway station, ride with you to Connecticut and explain my plan. I would travel back to New York City by mass transit and we would go our separate ways."

One of my faults is that I can be too trusting. I placed him on hold to give me time to make this critical decision.

My friends who heard half of the conversation were concerned about my safety and said I should not go. One friend was a volunteer and was on leave from her fulltime job in law enforcement. She advised me, "If you insist upon meeting with him, you should at least take a photo of him with your cell phone and send it back to us in the firehouse. Just in case the guy is an "Emotionally Disturbed Person" (EDP) or some other person with nefarious purposes."

I came back to the phone and said to my new friend, "Ok, let's meet at the south end of the Sheepshead Bay subway station in an

159

hour. I have a red Nissan and we should have plenty of time to discuss your plan."

At the pre-arranged time, I spotted him in the crowd walking down the stairs. He stood out from the others. He was tall, distinguished in appearance and well dressed. I flashed my lights to signal him my location. As he came closer, I began to notice an unusual glint in his eyes. I followed my friend's suggestion and quickly snapped a photo of him and forwarded it to the firehouse. He buckled in and we set out on our journey to Connecticut. Traffic was really bad and the trip would take over two hours.

Once in the car, we shook hands and he started the conversation, "Thank you for agreeing to meet me on such a short notice. I'm returning shortly to my country and we would've missed the opportunity to talk."

We crawled along the Eastbound Belt Parkway and made small talk to get to know each other. I wanted to save the serious conversation for when we were mired in the traffic of the Van Wyck Expressway. It would be easy to concentrate on what he said.

He was slightly older than myself and appeared to be well-educated. "In New Zealand I was a very successful car salesman and made my money in car dealerships." His professional demeanor reflected his successful career and it was obvious that he was highly educated. I shared with him my status, "At the time, our days are spent trying to get the firehouse fully operational while providing fire safety coverage to the community after our recent disaster. I really didn't know how I could help you or how you can help us."

I now began to realize that I made a terrible mistake by agreeing to meet with him. Allowing a stranger into my car, I unnecessarily put myself in an extremely dangerous situation with someone who was potentially unstable. Driving over the Whitestone Bridge, he began to reveal his plan. "I want to develop a 'coupon card system' that on a grand scale could be used to fund support for all global disasters. My plan calls for the development of a credit card-like system where accounts would be credited with funds when they utilized discount coupons for the purchase of a variety of products. It would require the manufacturer to be part of the program. Any coupon could be redeemed by crediting the coupon account and not by getting a credit refund at the store. I plan to allow a free registration but the cardholder would agree to a minimum monthly or yearly fee. This fee would be automatically withdrawn from the account. These funds would go to managing the program and the surplus would go to an international disaster relief fund. Any surplus funds would go to developing countries to help improve their resiliency. Right now, the global usage of regular credit cards is approaching 2.8 billion. Each card has a yearly fee ranging from fifty dollars to over one hundred."

His coupon idea when compared to the global credit card system now made partial sense but had many inherent problems when dealing with the details. The whole idea was way beyond my pay grade and would be years away from fruition. While his idea was interesting, I had many urgent issues staring me in the face, which required my immediate attention. My new dilemma was how honest was I going to be with him when he asked me for my thoughts?

The traffic was easing up as we approached the Connecticut border and he pointed out a sign for White Plains, New York. "My son and his family lives there in White Plains." It was a big surprise.

"Do you get to visit them on your trips to New York?" I asked.

"I haven't spoken to anyone in my family for nearly ten years."

I asked him why he was estranged from them and he gave me his chilling response. "It's all because of my obsession over this coupon credit card idea. I came up with the idea over a decade ago and my passion for it managed to alienate my entire family."

He quickly shifted his attention back to his sales pitch for the coupon cards. We were now on the Merritt Parkway with little traffic and it was now dark. I began to fear for my safety and was glad I sent the photo to my friends. His voice was rising and it was obvious that his agitation was increasing. He clenched his hands into fists and began to punch my car's dashboard. I did my best to calm him. "It's not a bad idea," I lied. I could see many problems with the concept, but

I assured him I thought it was a good idea. And like magic he calmed down. He felt I was an ally and not a foe. I asked him, "Why haven't you approached someone like Bill Gates or the TV show 'Shark Tank' instead of myself?" After Sandy, I was economically challenged. I lost my car and my house was uninhabitable and I had yet to learn what losses the insurance company would cover. I couldn't understand why he chose me to share his idea. "Someone like Bill Gates would be interested in helping and would have the financial resources to make it happen."

He told me, "I have tried numerous times with him and other billionaires from around the world and haven't been able to get past their initial screeners." As we were pulling into the Metro North Station near Wilton, Connecticut I asked him, "Why did you choose me to share your idea with?"

He told me, "For some reason, I knew you would listen. I hope that you will share it with someone who could make it happen." I promised him I would try.

At the train station we shook hands and before parting our ways he thanked me profusely for just taking the time to listen. This was proof that one kind word can change someone's day. I regret not asking him why he was so absorbed with this idea. Did he experience some natural disaster and was he financially ruined? I'll never know. During most of our conversation, I was anticipating what I would do if he became fully emotionally deranged. I was currently absorbed with restoring the PBFD, the Breezy Point community and the Rockaway peninsula after the superstorm. He was absorbed with creating a global plan to help everyone negatively impacted by all kinds of disasters. His idea caused him to be alienated from his family and friends. His idea was destroying himself. I made a promise to myself not to let that happen to me. I often wondered how he knew I would take the time to listen. Maybe because of his disaster experience, he knew that after experiencing a disaster many of us were highly vulnerable. As survivors we wanted to find ways to quickly recover and help others to lessen their burdens in future disasters. Unlike some others, he was not an evil person looking only to take advantage of someone. But like some of the other people I experienced, he didn't come easy.

We had many calls from well-meaning people with grandiose plans and were able to screen them in advance. However, my vulnerability in getting involved with some questionable people continued. One of the calls touched upon an idea that I independently developed. In my idle moments after Sandy, I kept focusing upon alternate methods of throwing water at a fire inside of a hurricane. In the future all newly built homes would require an independent sprinkler system for each house. In a multi-residential fire this would create an additional burden to the water supply. Drafting in a seaside community had its inherent problems with sea shell particles contaminating a pump. Could we do something different other than resorting to a "bucket brigade?" Coincidentally, while on a vacation, I saw a person enjoying a ride from a new recreational gadget attached to a jet ski. The rider was being lifted more than 10 feet out of the water using the redirected thrust from the jet ski's propulsion system. I surmised if the Jet Ski's water could be diverted to go through a nozzle, it could be used as a mobile vehicle to throw water on a fire. It would be like a mini fireboat and would be ideal to use in a situation like we experienced. There would be problems with debris clogging filters but with proper engineering it might be possible to minimize or eliminate these problems.

Ironically, I received a call from a Canadian who had a similar idea. We talked at great length over several months. We developed a plan to establish an enterprise that would address this issue. After giving him several thousand dollars of my own money, without any results, I became suspicious of the operation. I called a friend and financial advisor to look into the situation and to speak with my contact. In a short time, he advised me not to send any additional money and to disengage from any and all business dealings. He said there were many scams related to post-disaster situations. He politely let me know that I was most likely scammed and should cease and desist. It was great advice and any money I lost I chalked up to tuition in the school of hard knocks. In the disaster response world, it's difficult to make long-term changes. It doesn't come easy.

Nearly a year after Superstorm Sandy, I was appointed as an honorary battalion chief in the FDNY's Honorary Fire Officer's Association. I was sworn in by Commissioner Cassano; and Chief Kilduff, chief of the department held the Bible. It was a special honor because I think very few New York City Volunteer Firefighters are selected. They gave me an identification card, badge and a lapel pin. Jokingly, the chief said not to use the badge to get out of a traffic ticket. Several months later, I met a person attending a dinner in New York City. After shaking my hand, he spotted my honorary fire officer's lapel pin. "What is that pin for?" he asked. I had never met this individual and later discovered that he had a reputation for being toxic and abrasive. I explained to him, "I was recognized by the FDNY and made an honorary battalion fire chief."

"How did you get that honor?" he asked.

I told him, "I was the PBFD Fire Chief during the Hurricane Sandy six-alarm fire at Breezy Point."

He responded, "Why did they give that to you? You lost over one-hundred and thirty homes."

I was in shock, and his five surrounding friends had their heads down with obvious expressions of embarrassment. Not since high school did I have such an urge to punch someone in the face. Sticks and stones can break my bones but words can deliver a bitter blow. I maintained my cool, exercised great restraint, and politely said to him, "You just stabbed me in the heart. We stopped the westward advancement of the fire and prevented nearly two thousand homes from being destroyed. We are most proud of the fact that no one died during Sandy in Breezy Point."

I abruptly left him and reminded myself of the great moment when the homeowners from the fire zone gave me and the PBFD the standing ovation at their town hall meeting. His comments were inaccurate, unnecessary and annoying. There is Karma in this world. Two years later he was arrested and charged with DWI but I still keep him in my prayers. Again, it doesn't come easy.

CHAPTER 13

The Good News Story

MANY PEOPLE WANTED to hear our story of how we sheltered in place in the face of Superstorm Sandy. How, in the event of a fire, we prepared ourselves to fight inside a hurricane. And many also wanted to hear about our "prayer huddles." Our broken-down firehouse became a symbol of an unbroken will to support a devastated community. We were visited by domestic and international film crews from the UK, China and along the way we hosted a group of fire chiefs from Japan. The Japanese Fire Chiefs heard about our disaster and wanted to see our burn zone and hear us tell our story. They looked like traditional Japanese Samurai warriors, as they listened intently to

Japanese fire chiefs visiting PBFD.

my translated remarks. They were very impressed how our volunteer organizations worked so well with the FDNY.

President Obama did a low fly-by of our area and the Prime Minister of Ireland (The Taoiseach) also visited the community. He attended a Mass in our church and was asked to do one of the scripture readings. The Irish Consulate General to New York, who also served as the Irish Ambassador to the UN, visited Breezy Point earlier and actually helped one of our neighbors shovel sand out of his basement. I overheard the Taoiseach and the ambassador say how amazed they were that everyone they met in Breezy looked like people they knew from their home. Breezy Point was primarily an Irish neighborhood, populated with descendants of Irish immigrants. It was an honor that they chose this time to support us. Their visit was spectacular and I'm sure our ancestors were smiling down upon them in appreciation of this simple gesture.

Irish Consulate General and Irish Ambassador to the U.N., Noel Kilkenny, lending a helping hand.

Many church groups wanted to hear from us firsthand about the prayer huddles. I had attended a dinner in Manhattan and was seated next to the mother of a New York Giants football player. She told me that she was the Pastor of Gold Hill Baptist Church in Stanley, North Carolina. After sharing with her our story, she invited me to speak to her congregation. It was exciting to be there as a guest and an honor to stand at their altar preaching our "Good News Story." The painting of the Miracle Trucks of Breezy Point from the pastor of a church in Jamaica, New York has moved many people.

I was asked to speak at the annual dinner of the Ligonier, Pennsylvania, Volunteer Fire Department. I spoke about our miracles and how the volunteer fire community supported our recovery efforts. The mix of volunteers from all over the country helped to create a "universal firehouse." We shared stories and learned firefighting techniques from each other that improved our professionalism. Our story resonated worldwide within the firefighting and religious worlds.

We used this momentary fame to help raise funds and financially prepare us for the purchase of a new fire truck. I tasked Firefighter Chris Warren to be in charge of sales for our new line of apparel. In his full-time career, he was a music teacher for the New York City Department of Education. He recruited his father, who was a past chief of the PBFD to work with him on this project. They traveled with us to our speaking engagements and set up shop for their sales operation. He was also very computer savvy and set up a mail order system. My son's girlfriend, Maureen, was highly skilled as an artist and she designed several of the PBFD shirts and hats. She linked up with a company that manufactured the clothing. Chris Warren also convinced his mother to turn her garage and part of her living room into a storage room for our extra stock. In a few short months, Chris and his father raised nearly $30,000 from their sales. This was money that was desperately needed for our reconstruction efforts and for the purchase of a new truck.

One of my friends in the 88th was a first generation Chinese-American. When he was younger, he and his parents emigrated from

China to the United States. He grew up speaking Chinese and as an adult he became a businessman with frequent trips to China. After I learned that China Central TV (CCTV) wanted to do an interview on our Sandy Disaster experience, I met with him to get some background in preparation for the meeting with the Chinese Press. After telling him that CCTV wanted to interview me in regard to Hurricane Sandy, he told me I had it all wrong. He said CCTV covers all of China and has news outlets all over the globe. He said that CCTV is too big and they would not be interested in doing a news story on Breezy Point and Hurricane Sandy. I again assured him that this was not a prank and I gave him the name of the Chinese reporter I planned to do the interview with. His face was in shock and he said she is a big news personality in China and she couldn't be doing the story. He finally accepted my explanation and gave me some helpful background information.

I was aware that China was a Communist country and as such they didn't support religion but rather propagated atheism in their society. Because of this I decided to skip over the part where we conducted our prayer huddles and witnessed the three positive outcomes which were really miracles.

On the day of the interview, she was accompanied by another female CCTV reporter who was based in New York. The New York based reporter was fluent in English, whereas the lady from mainland China had a weaker grasp of the language. Of course, my understanding of Chinese was non-existent and my vocabulary consisted of one word. They were also accompanied by a contracted cameraman from Boston whose assignment was to video the interviews. The meeting with the press started inside the firehouse and they were able to video some of our members from the night shift catching some sleep. We had several US flags that were battered from Sandy and were hanging indoors covering up the holes in our walls. The scene was an accurate portrayal of our shabby existence in the shadow of Manhattan. The camera team really seemed to focus on our exhausted firefighters and battered flags as if we were brutally defeated.

As our story progressed, I showed the crew the path we followed when we abandoned the firehouse and brought the reporter to the side door of the clubhouse. As I opened the door, she looked inside and I could tell she recognized the interior of the building. Evidently, she must have reviewed file video in advance of her visit. She immediately turned to me and in an almost angry voice she asked me, "Is this the place where you said the prayers?"

I was shocked and almost speechless. The camera was still rolling and I knew I had to respond. Very politely I said, "Yes, it is, ma'am." I actually thought that there would not be any follow-up questions on the subject but she proved me wrong. In a near angry staccato voice where each word was sharply detached from the others, she asked me, "Why did you say these prayers?"

In an unfiltered and almost innocent way I responded, "Because it works. You guys should try it."

I almost regretted my comments but this was New York and honest answers were commonplace. I knew the camera caught the exchange but somehow during the editing process those frames would end up on the editor's floor. We became friends during the rest of the filming and when the story aired, she was kind enough to send me a CD copy of the story. I was not surprised to see that the prayer comments were not included. I was happy that our story was carried to faraway lands and shared with millions of the Chinese people.

Through our PBFD website I was contacted by a documentary filmmaker and producer from Holland. He was doing a documentary on global warming and wanted to include our experience of fighting a fire inside Superstorm Sandy. I was hesitant to do the interview and didn't want to get caught in any political crossfire about global warming or climate change. I know that we have temperature records for the last 150 years and can reconstruct weather over the past 1,000 years. Scientists know that the Ice Age began 2.4 million years ago and ended 11,500 years ago. Personally, I am undecided if our current global weather is due to manmade conditions or if it is part of a normal cycle. I am a firm believer that we need to be good stewards of the environment. We need to leave a healthy environment for the next generations and they need to do the same. I am happy about the success of the United States Environmental Protection Agency (EPA) and the United Nations Environment Programme (UNEP). Air quality has certainly improved and we are moving in the right direction with improving vehicular air emissions.

This documentary film maker was concerned about global warming contributing to more frequent and stronger hurricanes. They were also concerned about the polar ice cap melting, warmer ocean temperature and rising sea levels. I knew with my combined lifetime experience in the air rescue business, the disaster response business and now the firematic experience, that we were encountering storms of greater intensity and more frequency. It didn't matter to me if it was "climate change" or a cyclic event causing "global warming." Something big was happening.

It is widely known that hurricanes gain strength from warm waters. The oceans cover about seventy percent of the earth's surface. When the hurricanes make landfall, they lose strength because they become separated from their energy source in the water and because of increased surface friction on land. The water surface acts like a giant solar panel and absorbs the direct sunlight. In late spring and summer, the days are longer and the sun heats the water at varying depths. A thermocline is created when the heated surface water meets a temperature gradient with a steep drop off of temperature. This area of heated surface water to the thermocline is called the fuel tank and its depth varies with the amount of sunlight and ambient temperature. In the lower latitudes this area can become quite deep whereas around the polar caps it could be non-existent. Meteorologists use the size of the fuel tank as one of their indicators in making predictions for the upcoming hurricane season.

I spent nearly a day with the Dutch filmmaker and when finished I felt that it did not go well. Once he heard that I was undecided about "global warming" or weather cycles he seemed to lose interest in my contributions. I think he missed my point. Whether this was a warm age following the ice age or global warming from our mismanagement we need to do something about it. With deeper fuel tanks in our oceans, we will see more frequent and stronger hurricanes traveling further north. Each year we spend billions for disaster recovery on a global basis for damage from hurricanes. Maybe we can bring together some of the world's great minds to develop a more proactive approach to limit the damage from these storms. Our efforts to gain resiliency after each storm is good but how can we be proactive? In the old days we seeded clouds with silver oxide crystals to reduce a storm's impact. Could we develop an environmentally friendly method to reduce the size of the "Fuel Tank," to deny these embryonic storms their much-needed fuel? Mark Twain frequently used the expression; "Everybody complains about the weather, but nobody does anything about it."

I never heard from this film crew again and I strongly suspect my comments were edited. At least I can say it won't be the first time that my comments ended up on the editing floor.

The "Good News story" continued with an interview by NBC News Washington for their Six O'clock News Edition. We had a great interview with Sam Champion of ABC News and did a film tour of the devastated area for their Hurricane Sandy segment. The Weather Channel did an entire episode on Sandy and keeping with their format, they would hire real actors to play the part of the key people within the story. I, of course, thought they were going to get someone like George Clooney to play my part, but instead, the actor they chose appeared to be fifteen years older than me. He didn't come close to the self-image I carried of myself and he looked like he couldn't make any decision, much less find his way out of a paper bag!

I was invited to speak at a rather large gathering of the Putnam County Volunteer Fire Department training event in eastern New York State and worked with the Fireman's Association of the State of New York (FASNY) and the Volunteer Fireman Insurance Service (VFIS). Chief John Sroka of the New York State Fire Chiefs Association accompanied me. Again, we shared valuable information gained during the whole experience. The group was very attentive and listened and seemed to hang on each and every word. It was during this time that I began to notice that, at times, I would feel overwhelmed reliving the experience and my voice would start breaking up. I knew the pressure of the entire experience was starting to have a negative effect on me personally.

For a small volunteer fire department in a major city some would say we received "a lot of ink" for our accomplishments. I am humbled to be part of the global firematic community who routinely accomplish greater deeds on a daily basis. Our "Good News story" is a part of that bigger story which often goes unknown. I would hope that by sharing our story many in the career field could also be honored. Special honors should go to the Rockaway Point and Roxbury Volunteer Fire Departments and the FDNY. They stood beside us that night and later became pillars of strength for our community in our recovery phase. When together, we would all agree that "we were just doing our job." I would hope that our good news story could also be used by others as a template in their preparation for future disasters.

CHAPTER 14

Epilogue

SOME SAY THAT if you live near the ocean someday a wave will come along and knock you down. For the people of Breezy Point and other coastal communities of New York City, Superstorm Sandy was that wave. It was not just a wave but "the Perfect Storm." It led us on a journey into disaster and through our persistence and the generous help of many strangers we returned stronger than before. Like the mythological bird "the Phoenix" we were able to find renewal and re-birth but it came with a price. In the end. the water that we loved and the cause of our attraction to the area, became our most dangerous foe.

During my speech with the Columbiettes, an auxiliary of the Knights of Columbus I had a near breakdown experience. Halfway through, my voice became wobbly and tears started to roll off my face and I became very emotional. I looked into the crowd and they became quiet. Most likely, they were embarrassed for me.

Let the Restoration of Homes and Hearts Begin!!

It looked like some of the audience was feeling the emotion as well and were starting to cry on their own. A young firefighter, Tom Nestor who is nicknamed the "Mayor of Breezy Point," seriously considered helping me out by taking the microphone. He comes from a family where generations of his relatives have a proud record of service in the PBFD. Fortunately, I was able to finish the presentation in my emotional state. It would be the last time I spoke in public about Sandy and the PBFD. On the way out, my brother John pulled me aside and suggested I might have a touch of Post-Traumatic Stress Disorder (PTSD), but I will never know for sure. I did know the first anniversary of the storm was nearing and as I looked back, I began to understand why I lost my composure. Besides being the fire chief, it was as if I assumed too many hats of responsibility. In order to survive and rebuild we developed "franchises" that would help us get there. Our first was during the night of the storm. We created a public shelter, and after that we ran a disaster distribution center in the clubhouse. We became a donation center for food, clothes and cleaning supplies. Later, we became web-site managers and ran a communication center with our emails. We also created a "used fire truck sales department" from surplus donated used fire trucks. We set up a PBFD apparel shop and worked many mail orders. We also organized ourselves into a public relations entity and worked many news media, documentary film and public speaking events. We worked and helped spawn a newly created organization called, "Gut and Pump" and supported them with surplus tool donations that in turn were loaned to members of the community. We also developed construction work crews that helped to rebuild the firehouse, homes of our firefighters and our neighbors. Most importantly, we worked with others to clear the sand lanes of debris so we guaranteed access in the event of an emergency. Lastly, we provided organizational representation to the daily Breezy Point Cooperative and FEMA management meetings. All of these efforts contributed to regaining our financial situation and helped our neighbors to complete their recovery.

I was not the only guy feeling the strain; other members were also experiencing the similar feelings. Because of the great amount of time spent at the firehouse and the resultant stress, several of our team experienced serious trouble in long term personal relationships. Past Chief Ed Wolfe was a great asset and traveled with me on several fund-raising events. We were friends before but Sandy brought us very close. He died suddenly of a heart attack. He died too young and his passing rocked our world. I take comfort in the book of Luke 23:43 knowing that Ed will be with the Lord in paradise.

Several members were fortunate to have passed the FDNY civil service test and were appointed to be probationary firefighters. It was a lifetime dream and the PBFD helped them to get there. The ultimate irony was that there was some long-time friction between the full-time paid firefighters and the non-paid volunteer firefighters. Some of it was legitimate, since many of the volunteers came across as "Buffs" and successfully managed to alienate themselves. When the members of the "core group" entered their "probie class" and arrived at their first assignment, they instinctively knew not to discuss their experience. I later found out that one of them actually denied knowing me. I fully understood and didn't have any angst. With all of us going in different directions, I find myself in the role of a cheerleader, standing on the sidelines and rooting for them as they progress in their careers. They know that I'm there for them. It is a lifetime commitment.

The firehouse is up and running and in better shape than before. We now have an industrial grade kitchen and have installed a shower and a washer and dryer. This will help us if we are faced with another long term "shelter in place" tasking. We have a new generator that is raised beyond flood expectations and we have elevated all of the electrical service to survive another biblical flood. Our alarm system is new and modern as well as our portable radios. Our new fire truck with improved design is working like a charm. Our plans for a second floor to gain improved training classrooms and a bunk room have slowly moved forward. It would never be fast enough for me. Some think the return of Superstorm Sandy is 700 years away. I think it can happen a lot sooner. Our current hydrant system needs to be updated to avoid some of the low water pressure conditions we experienced.

The community has also risen from the ashes. It is very difficult to identify the "fire zone." Because all of the new homes are elevated and equipped with sprinklers, some people are calling the area "Breezy Heights." Steve Greenberg and some other prominent residents created the Breezy Point Disaster Relief Fund and raised money to help our neighbors who were

Better days ahead for Breezy.

financially challenged after Sandy. The good people of Breezy Point returned to their generous ways of helping others. They rejoined those quiet and anonymous angels who swarm those in need after a disaster. They prefer to be on the giving end over the receiving end.

Up and down the entire peninsula there were so many examples of outstanding situational leadership and courage. Belle Harbor had a similar fire and two young surfers braved the icy waters and rescued stranded people on their surfboards. Their surfboards became a lightweight improvised rescue vehicle. Dylan Smith and Michael McDonnell did an outstanding job of rescuing many people. Sadly, their young lives were shortened after the dust from Sandy settled. I'm sure they are in a special place in Heaven. In Breezy Point, Cathy Brennan's son did the same thing and rescued many people. There are many stories of local heroism and they could be heard in the quiet conversations at the local pubs.

The Breezy Point Cooperative, with their own resources, built a barrier system of sand dunes to make the community more resilient for future events. The co-op's former manager, Mr. Arthur Lighthall, did a yeoman's job in bringing the community back. Our three volunteer fire departments are continuing with their traditions that have guarded the community over the last hundred years. Our recruitment efforts continue. In a world of computer technology, it is difficult to get young people to leave their comfortable environments exploring cyberspace to join an organization that trains you how to save lives and run into burning buildings.

Along the way we met and became life-long friends with a variety of people. Mike and Judy Scotko said that during one afternoon, as they stood on the remnants of their shattered deck, they were greeted by Marines and Mormons and were asked, "Hello, what can we do to help." We were also visited by the Buddhists who handed out an endless supply of gift cards. Habitat for Humanity, Operation Blessing, Catholic Charities and work crews from major corporations gave us their help and expertise. One construction company loaned us a large industrial strength generator that kept the PBFD running until electricity was restored. I met with several Amish Firefighters. Underneath their straw hats and behind their intense eyes, I knew we were both members of the same special group that dedicate themselves to their community. I was honored by their presence and thanked them for taking the time to help us in our time of need. Besides the Amish Firefighters, we had volunteer firefighters from all over the country and we became the "universal firehouse." Seventy-five percent of all firefighters in the United States and Canada are volunteers. It was a tremendous experience.

Superstorm Sandy taught us to keep going and not to dwell on our misfortunes. Houses can be rebuilt but people can't. Sandy also reminded us that life is precious and family is most important. All of us stepped away from this experience with a greater respect for "Mother Nature" and many of us reinforced our beliefs in God and the power of prayer. Some people falsely believe this is a "seven-hundred-year storm" and nothing will happen again. We can't in our lifetimes fool ourselves and think that this will never happen again.

From my chief's perspective, I think our key strength both during the storm and on the long road to recovery was the decision-making process. At times, especially during the storm and fire, we were faced with many challenges that required making complicated decisions in a short time. I was fortunate that I was surrounded by a very competent team who offered timely and valuable input. After listening to them and considering their input, combined with my lifetime experience, I was able to successfully make decisions that helped us to accomplish the mission and recover fully. I am eternally grateful for their support and I'm confident that we would not be

One of the many Amish firefighters who came to our assistance.

where we are today without our teamwork. During the August 2013 annual business meeting I stepped down as chief and looked forward to my own down time. Chief John Fahy became my successor and continued to carry on with the PBFD traditions.

In my idle moments during the recovery phase, some of my Superstorm Sandy stories would bubble up and I'd share them with my fellow members of the PBFD. My good friend, Tim O'Regan, constantly suggested that I write a book. Ever since my last speech at the Knights of Columbus, when I discovered I had a touch of PTSD, I also had a strong case of writer's block. Despite Tim's persistent efforts I never put pen to paper. Perhaps the greatest irony is that it took another disaster, the COVID-19 Pandemic, to motivate me to break down the writer's block wall. During the pandemic quarantine I was able to focus and produce a story that needs to be told. I look forward to the day when Sandy is a distant memory and when someone says, "Sandy? Who is she?"

APPENDIX I

HISTORY OF THE POINT BREEZE VOLUNTEER FIRE DEPARTMENT, INC.

THE POINT BREEZE Volunteer Fire Department Inc, is incorporated as a fire department by the State of New York. It is situated in Breezy Point, which is located on the western tip of the Rockaway Peninsula in Queens County, New York. Established in 1910, it is one of nine volunteer fire departments within the City of New York. The Point Breeze Volunteer Fire Department is financially self-sustaining through community support and public grants.

In 1977, attorney John Ingram did the necessary paperwork to incorporate the organization as a fire department under the State of New York. The charter was signed by Mayor Abe Beame as a volunteer fire department and filed on December 30, 1977. The incorporators were Kevin Whalen Sr., Michael Schramm, Sr. and Walter Uhlig.

The first firehouse was on Hillcrest Walk facing the bay near Point Breeze Avenue. It was a wooden structure built above the sand to create storage space underneath. It contained two hose reels and a large mounted CO_2 extinguisher, all of which had to be pulled on a cart manually by the members to the scene of the fire.

There was a large bell tower next to the firehouse. In the event of a fire, a volunteer would strike the bell with a mallet several times. The volunteers were each given a whistle to alert the community of a fire by blowing three times on the whistle. This was the first use of three blasts for a fire, a tradition that continues today to alert the community and call volunteers to the firehouse. Several hand-cranked sirens were located throughout the Breezy community. An alarm for fire could be sent out by anyone in the community.

Once assembled, the members pulled the hose to a water outlet. The first hydrants were 2-inch standpipes to which the hoses were attached. This was a shaky operation at best due to little or no water pressure. Some of these standpipes can still be seen around the beach. At the beginning of the summer, large water-can fire extinguishers were placed in wooden boxes attached to poles in strategic areas. They were taken in and stored in the firehouse at the end of the summer and serviced the next spring. It should be noted that the department only operated in the summer months because Breezy Point was at that time only a summer community.

In 1926, the modern fire hydrants were put into operation. There were seven of them around the beach. By the early 1940s the standpipes were taken out of service. The water flow to Breezy Point gradually increased over the years. Roxbury continued to have standpipes connected to underground wells which were scattered throughout the community. Roxbury did away with their wells in the 1970s.

In 1938, a wooden firehouse was built at 332 Point Breeze Avenue. It remained as the quarters until 1975. The current home of the Point Breeze Volunteer Fire Department, which is over 35 years old, suits all of the needs of a modern fire department. In 1975 Tom Ingram was the architect for the firehouse which cost $50,000 for the bare-bones construction.

Over the years the department has had an interesting array of fire apparatus. As previously stated, in the early years hand carts were used to pull hoses to the scene of a fire which was a very difficult task. The department purchased a Cadillac and a LaSalle hearse from which the backs were removed and flatbeds installed to carry the hose.

The first actual fire engine was a 1925 Mack, which arrived in Breezy in 1948. This was a chain-driven vehicle, which could not operate in the sand and remained in service until 1958. I can recall that if it failed to start with the ignition key, it had a hand crank to crank the engine. The "Sand Flea I" was a converted World War II weapons carrier. The members of the department bought it for $750 in 1952. This small fire truck remained in service until 1964. In 1958, a 1941 Mack was purchased to replace the 1925 Mack. This truck, a favorite among the older members because of its savvy appearance, remained in service until 1967. "Sand Flea II" was the first fire apparatus purchased new in Breezy Point, arriving in 1964. Its small size and maneuverability in the sand made it the workhorse of the department until it was taken out of service in late 1984. While plans were underway for a large custom-made truck in the late sixties, a 1947 Ford was pressed into action as an interim truck. It remained for just two years, until "Big Jack" arrived in 1970. The "Big Jack," a 1969 GMC, was by far the most complete and flexible piece of fire apparatus in service at the time.

In 1984, the "Sand Flea III" arrived. This truck brought with it many new advances in firefighting equipment. It had a 1,000-gallon-per-minute pump and 1,000 feet of 5-inch supply line. This, along with a 20-inch water main supply system and 144 hydrants, afforded the residents of Breezy Point, Rockaway Point, and Roxbury an excellent fire protection system. In April of 1993, the Big Jack was taken out of service after twenty-three years of service. As an interim replacement, while a new apparatus was being built, the department received a 1979 GMC from the Melville Fire Department – thanks to Mike McKeefrey. This rig operated strictly as a truck company because it did not have a pump.

In October 1994, Point Breeze received its newest piece of apparatus, a 1994 International Truck built by KME. It was equipped with a 750-gallon-per-minute pump. In 2010, Unit 7, the 1984 International Pumper, a 25-year-old workhorse, was replaced by a 2010 International Truck built by KME. This new truck – "BIG JACK" named after our late and former Chief Jack Crowley – carries nine firefighters including the chauffeur and MPO and officer or senior man.

The area protected by the Point Breeze Volunteer Fire Department is geographically challenging. The Breezy Point Cooperative is a residential community of 2,862 homes, surrounded on two sides by the Atlantic Ocean and on one side by the Rockaway Inlet (Jamaica Bay). Most of the residential homes are located in the sand and can only be reached via sand lanes with four-wheel drive apparatus. To ensure appropriate fire protection for its residents, the department currently maintains two four-wheel drive engines with front-mounted pumps. Over the years, the department has maintained and serviced all of its emergency equipment to keep it in good operational condition, but over time all equipment needs to be replaced. We acquired a new engine in 2011.

The department has assisted in several marine rescue operations including the rescue of the crew and illegal immigrants on the Motor Vessel GOLDEN VENTURE which grounded about 500 yards off Fort Tilden in Gateway National Park in May 1993. More than 300 illegal Chinese immigrants and crew were rescued, and unfortunately ten people died from drowning. The department has also been involved over the years with the rescue of stranded fishermen on the rock jetty at the western tip of Breezy Point, referred to by residents as "the rocks." The department has responded to other vessels in distress.

Breezy Point is situated approximately 15 miles due south of the World Trade Center and on September 11, 2001, the department was called upon by the FDNY Dispatcher to relocate and provide firefighters and rig to FDNY Firehouse (Engine 266) while their company relocated to respond to rescue/recovery efforts at the Trade Center. The department's firefighters also responded to the World Trade Center, assisting in rescue/recovery efforts for fellow FDNY brothers, police, and citizens.

On November 12, 2001, the department was called upon once again with the crash of American Airlines Flight 587 in Belle Harbor, approximately three miles from the firehouse. They were the second fire company to arrive at the scene and they knocked down two house fires.

Every day the department's 40 members are responsible for protecting and serving the community, which is faced with new challenges in the twenty-first century. Today the Point Breeze Fire Department, which began full-time, year-round operation in 1959, responds to over 125 calls a year. There are a variety of emergencies such as brush, car, and structure fires; car accidents; floods; storm-related accidents; sparking and downed wires; boats in distress; and blackouts. Recently we have had a rash of gas leaks.

Over the years there have been 38 chiefs and 1,000 members. We have been the training academy for many of the FDNY's Bravest. With continued community support and an influx of brave new members to fill the ranks, the Point Breeze Volunteer Fire Department will be equipped to serve and protect the Breezy Point Cooperative into the next century.

"On October 29, 2012, Hurricane Sandy struck Breezy Point, home to many New York City first responders. Firefighters from the Roxbury, Rockaway Point, and Point Breeze Volunteer Fire Departments remained on duty throughout the storm, ready to assist our neighbors. That night, our quiet oceanfront community was ravaged by the hurricane's winds and waves, leaving 202 homes destroyed and 2,219 severely damaged. Another 135 homes were then devoured by one of the largest residential fires in New York City history." For a more detailed account, please see the Battle for Breezy Point by Sebastian Danese, and *Flood, Fire and a Superstorm* by Marty Ingram.

The department acquired a new truck in 2016. The department is always looking for new volunteers to carry on the long tradition of citizen-firefighter.